SOUTH VIETNAM
A POLITICAL HISTORY
1954–1970

SOUTH VIETNAM: a political history, 1954–1970, by Keesing's contemporary archives. Scribner, 1970. 168p map (Keesing's
research report, 5) 70-134360. 5.95, 2.95 pa.
As essential to any library as the *Keesing's contemporary archives* file
itself. In the maze of coups and counter-coups with which South
Viet-Nam was saddled in the mid-sixties, it was difficult to keep clarity
about the sequence of events or the exact order of succession of individuals in office. The present volume has dexterously combined chronol-
ogy and documentation for the confusing period of Vietnamese history
since Dien Bien Phu. It should be an invaluable guide for any re-
searcher in the field. A valuable index listing all the important
personalities in Vietnamese politics with a brief description of their
official position.

CHOICE   *MAY '71*

History, Geography &
Travel

Asia & Oceania

KEESING'S RESEARCH REPORT

SOUTH VIETNAM
A POLITICAL HISTORY
1954–1970

CHARLES SCRIBNER'S SONS
New York

CONTENTS

for Peace – Dismissal of Admiral Chung Tan Cang – Dissolution of Armed Forces Council – Resignation of Government – Military Junta takes Power – Cabinet Changes

The Historical Background

After 1,000 years of Chinese domination the Empire of Vietnam attained its independence in 939, although it nominally remained a tributary State of China. Originally confined to the Red River delta area, the Empire gradually expanded southward until it reached the Gulf of Siam in the 18th century. Christian missionary activity, carried on particularly by French priests, began in the 17th century, and despite recurrent outbursts of persecution resulted in the establishment of a large Vietnamese Catholic community.

The murder of French missionaries led to armed intervention in 1859 by a French force, which occupied Saigon and three adjacent provinces. The remainder of Cochin China (South Vietnam) was annexed in 1867. After a new war in 1883 Tonkin (North Vietnam) and Annam (Central Vietnam) became French protectorates, and in 1887 were united with the French colony of Cochin China and the Kingdoms of Laos and Cambodia (also French protectorates) in the Indo-Chinese Union. Guerrilla resistance to French domination continued until 1916 under the leadership of members of the imperial family and the mandarin class.

Many underground nationalist organizations were formed in the 1920s, and in 1930 the Indo-Chinese Communist Party was founded by Nguyen Tat Thanh, who later adopted the revolutionary *nom de guerre* of Ho Chi

1

Minh. A nationalist uprising in Tonkin in 1930 was followed by a peasant revolt under Communist leadership, both rebellions being harshly repressed by the French. Two religious movements which originated during this period—the Cao Dai (a sect founded in 1919 as a synthesis of Christianity, Buddhism and other religions) and the Hoa Hao (a sect founded in 1939 and preaching a simplified form of Buddhism)—also developed strong nationalist overtones, and in consequence were persecuted by the French authorities.

Japanese forces occupied Vietnam in 1940, and in March 1945 ousted the French authorities and established a puppet regime headed by the Emperor Bao Dai. Ho Chi Minh had meanwhile established the Vietminh (Revolutionary League for the Independence of Vietnam) in China in 1941 as an alliance of Communist and nationalist organizations, and Vietminh bands carried on a guerrilla resistance to the Japanese, with some assistance from the U.S. military authorities. After the surrender of Japan in August 1945 the Vietminh took over Hanoi and Saigon; Bao Dai abdicated, and the Democratic Republic of Vietnam was established on Sept. 2, with Ho Chi Minh as President and Hanoi as its capital.

Under the Potsdam Agreement concluded by the U.S.A., Britain and the Soviet Union at the end of World War II in 1945, Vietnam was temporarily divided into two zones, the North being occupied by Chinese and the South by British troops. Whereas the Chinese recognized the Hanoi Government, the British military authorities refused to do so and rearmed the French troops interned by the Japanese, who seized control of Saigon. General elections to the National Assembly organized by the Vietminh had to be held clandestinely in the British zone.

A compromise agreement between the French and Vietnamese Governments was signed on March 6, 1946. The Democratic Republic of Vietnam was recognized as a free State forming part of the French Union; the reunion of Cochin China with Vietnam was to be submitted to a referendum; and French troops were to replace the Chinese in the northern zone. Repeated clashes occurred between the French and Vietnamese forces, however, and on Nov. 23 the French Navy bombarded Haiphong, killing 6,000 people. Ho Chi Minh's Government left Hanoi, and war began.

The French Government recognized Vietnam (including Cochin China) in 1949 as an independent State within the framework of the French Union, with Bao Dai as Chief of State and Saigon as its capital. Whilst the new State was granted diplomatic recognition by the Western Powers, the Communist countries officially recognized the Democratic Republic of Vietnam in 1950. U.S. military aid to the French war effort in Indo-China began in May 1950.

The Vietminh took the offensive in September 1950, and by the beginning of 1954 partly or wholly controlled almost all the rural areas of Tonkin and Annam, as well as large areas of Cochin China. The decisive battle of the war was fought at Dien Bien Phu, in north-west Tonkin, where after a siege lasting 55 days 10,000 French troops were forced to surrender on May 7, 1954. Peace negotiations opened in Geneva on the following day.

The Geneva Conference of 1954

Political developments immediately preceding, and during, the Geneva Conference

Franco–Vietnamese Negotiations

Negotiations for a new treaty between France and Vietnam, providing for Vietnam's complete independence within the French Union, opened in Paris on March 8, 1954.

At the first session on March 9, the Vietnamese delegation, which included Prince Buu Loc (Vietnamese Prime Minister), demanded the conclusion of two separate treaties, the first of which would recognize Vietnam's total independence, whilst the second would lay down conditions for Vietnam's future association with France.

In view of the growing agitation in Vietnam for the election of a Vietnamese National Assembly, Prince Buu Loc left for Saigon on March 15. The negotiations, which continued in his absence, remained virtually deadlocked for nearly a month, owing to the Vietnamese delegation's refusal to accept membership of the French Union in its existing form.

3

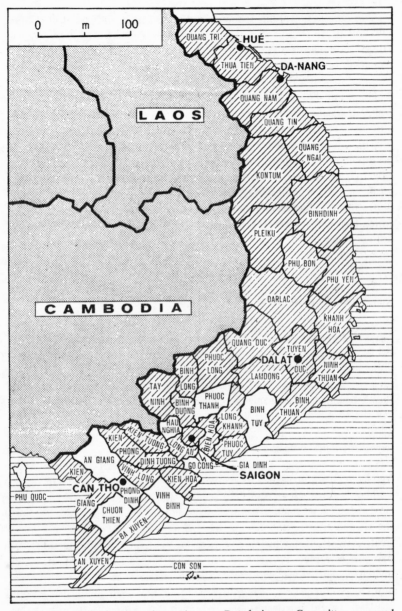

The provinces left blank are those where no Revolutionary Committee appeared
to have been set up at the time. Boundaries and names of provinces are those
used on maps published in Saigon and are not always identical with those used
by the Provisional Revolutionary Government.

(*Le Monde, July 31, 1969*)

On April 11 the Emperor Bao Dai arrived in France and as a result of subsequent private discussions with President Coty and M. Laniel (French Prime Minister) agreement was reached in principle that two treaties would be signed, fulfilling the demands of the Vietnamese delegation.

On April 25, however, Bao Dai's secretariat issued a communique complaining that Vietnam had not yet received adequate guarantees of her unity and independence, and suggesting that the French Government was prepared to accept a partition of Vietnam and to negotiate with the Vietminh without the consent of the Associated States. The French Government issued a statement later the same day expressing its astonishment at the Vietnamese communiqué, and pointing out that "the draft treaties of independence and association within the French Union, which have been drawn up by agreement between the two delegations, do not endanger the unity of Vietnam in any way and contain full guarantees for her independence."

The following joint declaration was issued on April 28 by M. Laniel and Nguyen Trung Vinh, the Vietnamese Vice-Premier:

"France, which remains faithful to the declaration of July 3, 1953, on the completion of Vietnam's independence, and Vietnam, which is resolved to maintain and consolidate the traditional friendship uniting her with the French people, affirm their agreement to regulate their mutual relations on the basis of two fundamental treaties. The first of these recognizes Vietnam's total independence and full and entire sovereignty. The second establishes a Franco-Vietnamese association within the French Union, based on equality and intended to develop co-operation between the two countries. Solemnly confirming their intention to carry out these two treaties, the Government of the French Republic and the Government of Vietnam agree to submit them simultaneously to the procedure of ratification provided for by their respective political systems."

Ngo Dinh Diem Succeeds Prince Buu Loc as Prime Minister

The Vietnamese Prime Minister, Prince Buu Loc, submitted his Government's resignation to the Emperor Bao Dai on June 16, 1954, on the ground that its mission had been fulfilled by the conclusion of the treaties of independence and association between Vietnam and France. Bao Dai accepted Prince Buu Loc's resignation and on the same day invited Ngo Dinh Diem, a leading Roman Catholic nationalist, to form a new Government.

5

Ngo Dinh Diem arrived in Saigon by air from Paris on June 25, and later the same day outlined his programme in a speech in which he promised to work for a lasting peace, "complete democracy and direct participation of the people in affairs of State," social reforms to improve the conditions of the peasantry and the working-class, the suppression of corruption, the complete independence of Vietnam, and national unity. Bao Dai announced on the same day that he had delegated full powers to the new Prime Minister to deal with the situation.

In the new Vietnamese Cabinet announced on July 5, Ngo Dinh Diem was Prime Minister and Minister of the Interior and Defence, and Dr. Tran Van Do Foreign Minister.

The Geneva Agreement of 1954

The Geneva Conference, which ended the First Indo-Chinese War, took place between May 8 and July 21, 1954, with the Foreign Ministers of the United Kingdom and the Soviet Union acting as co-chairmen. The other Governments represented were those of France, the State of Vietnam, the Democratic Republic of Vietnam, Cambodia, Laos, the U.S.A. and China.

Cease-Fire Agreement

A cease-fire agreement in respect of Vietnam (separate agreements were signed for Laos and Cambodia) was signed by the French and Vietminh commanders-in-chief on July 21, 1954. Its main provisions were as follows:

(1) A provisional military demarcation line would be fixed near the 17th parallel, the section to the north passing under the control of the Vietminh Government, that to the south remaining under the control of the Vietnamese Government. The Vietminh forces would be regrouped to the north and the French Union forces to the south of the line.

(2) A demilitarized zone, not more than five kilometers wide, would be established on either side of the demarcation line.

(3) Elections would be held simultaneously in both parts of Vietnam with the aim of establishing a unified Government.

(4) Both parties would refrain from reprisals and discrimination against persons or organizations on account of their activities during the hostilities.

(5) The introduction into Vietnam of reinforcements in men and material, and the establishment of new military bases, would be prohibited. Replacement of personnel and equipment might take place, however, under the supervision of the International Commission [see below].

(6) No military bases under the control of a foreign State might be established in

either zone, and the two parties would "ensure that the zones assigned to them do not adhere to any military alliance and are not used for the resumption of hostilities or to further an aggressive policy."

(7) All prisoners of war and civilian internees would be repatriated. Civilians residing in a district controlled by one party and wishing to live in the other zone would be permitted to make such a move during the period covered by the regrouping of troops.

(8) An International Commission, composed of representatives of Canada, India and Poland, and presided over by the Indian representative, would be set up to control and supervise the implementation of the armistice. Its recommendations would be made by majority vote, except when dealing with violations or threatened violations of the agreement which might lead to a resumption of hostilities, in which case its decisions would have to be unanimous.

The International Commission would fulfill the tasks of control, observation, inspection and investigation connected with the application of the armistice agreement. In particular it would control the movements of the armed forces of the two parties; supervise the demarcation lines between the regrouping areas, and also the demilitarized zones; control the release of prisoners of war and civilian internees; and supervise at ports and airfields and along the frontiers the execution of those provisions regulating the introduction of armed forces and military equipment into Vietnam. For these purposes both fixed and mobile inspection teams, composed of equal numbers of Canadian, Indian and Polish officers, would be appointed by the Commission.

Final Declaration

A final declaration, which was tacitly adopted but not signed by eight of the participants in the Conference, viz. France, the Soviet Union, the United Kingdom, the People's Republic of China, (South) Vietnam, Laos, Cambodia, and the Democratic Republic of Vietnam stated *inter alia:*

"The conference recognizes that the essential purpose of the agreement relating to Vietnam is to settle military questions with a view to ending hostilities, and that the military demarcation line should not in any way be interpreted as constituting a political or territorial boundary. It expresses its conviction that the execution of the provisions set out in the present declaration and in the agreement on the cessation of hostilities creates the necessary basis for the achievement in the near future of a political settlement in Vietnam.

"The conference declares that, so far as Vietnam is concerned, the settlement of political problems, effected on the basis of respect for the principles of independence, unity and territorial integrity, shall permit the Vietnamese people to enjoy the fundamental freedoms, guaranteed by democratic institutions, established as a result of free general elections by secret ballot. To ensure that sufficient progress in the restoration of peace has been made, and that all the necessary conditions obtain for free expression of the national will, general elections shall be held in July 1956 under the supervision of an International Commission composed of representatives of the member-States of the International Supervisory Commission, referred to in the agreements on the cessation of hostilities. Consultations will be held on this subject between the competent representative authorities of the two zones from July 1955 onwards."

It also stated that the members of the Conference would consult one another on questions referred to them by the International Control Commission respecting the observance of the cease-fire agreements.

U.S. Unilateral Declaration

The U.S. Government, which dissociated itself from the Final Declaration, issued a unilateral declaration in which it stated that it would refrain from threat or the use of force to disturb the cease-fire agreements, and would view any renewal of aggression in violation of the agreements with grave concern and as seriously threatening international peace and security.

The statement continued:

"In connexion with the statement in the declaration concerning free elections in Vietnam, my Government wishes to make clear its position, which it has expressed in a declaration made in Washington, on June 29, 1954 [by President Eisenhower and Mr. Winston Churchill], as follows: 'In the case of nations now divided against their will, we shall continue to seek to achieve unity through free elections, supervised by the U.N., to ensure that they are conducted fairly.'

"With respect to the statement made by the representative of the State of Vietnam [see below], the United States reiterates its traditional position that peoples are entitled to determine their own future and that it will not join in an arrangement which would hinder this. Nothing in this declaration is intended to, or does, indicate any departure from this traditional position."

South Vietnamese Declaration

The South Vietnamese Foreign Minister, Dr. Tran Van Do, had issued a declaration during the final stages of the Geneva Conference, setting forth his Government's objections to the cease-fire agreement.

This declaration, the text of which was issued on July 21, proposed:
(1) a cease-fire throughout Vietnam, without any demarcation line being drawn; (2) the regrouping of the forces of both sides in specified areas; (3) the disarming of all irregular forces; (4) the disarming of the Vietminh forces, and the simultaneous withdrawal of all foreign troops from Vietnam; (5) elections throughout Vietnam when, in the opinion of the U.N., security and order had been re-established.

After protesting against "the rejection of these proposals without examination", the Vietnamese declaration registered four "solemn protests", as follows:
(1) Against "the haste with which the armistice agreement has been concluded by the French and Vietminh High Commands," in which connexion it was stated that "many clauses of the agreement are of a nature which gravely compromises the political future of the Vietnamese people"
(2) Against "the fact that the armistice agreement abandons to the Vietminh

8

certain territories which are still occupied by Vietnamese troops and which are essential for the defence of Vietnam against further Communist expansionism".

(3) Against "the action of the French High Command in arrogating to itself the right, without prior consultation with the State of Vietnam, of fixing the date of future elections".

(4) Against "the manner in which the armistice has been concluded and the conditions of the armistice, which take no account of the aspirations of the Vietnamese people". It was added that the Vietnamese Government reserved "full liberty of action to safeguard the sacred rights of the people of Vietnam to territorial unity, national independence and liberty"

Nevertheless, the Government of Vietnam indicated that they would not oppose the implementation of the final agreement reached by the Geneva Conference [see above], even though they were strongly opposed to the partition of Vietnam.

I. CONSOLIDATION OF THE DIEM REGIME
– JULY 1954 TO AUGUST 1956

During the period immediately following the cease-fire of August 1954, the South Vietnamese Government's authority was confined to Saigon and a few other large towns, the greater part of the country being controlled by the Caodaist, Hoa Hao [see page 2] and Binh Xuyen [see below] sects through their private armies, or by the Vietminh through its political organizations. Although Bao Dai was supported by a section of the Army High Command and by the Binh Xuyen, his prestige and authority had been greatly weakened by his frequent and prolonged visits to France, where he had been living since April 1954. Ngo Dinh Diem was not supported by any organized political movement, and had aroused strong opposition by his autocratic methods, and in particular by his strict control of the Press. The most important of the numerous political parties, the Socialist Party and the Dai Viet (a nationalist organization with strong support in Annam), maintained a hostile attitude towards both Bao Dai and Ngo Dinh Diem.

The **Binh Xuyen,** originating as a gang of bandits and river pirates, supported the Vietminh for a time, and in 1948 was granted control by the French of a zone between Saigon and the sea. By an arrangement with Bao Dai, it also secured control in 1954 of both the Saigon police and the national security police, as well as a monopoly of the gaming houses, opium dens and brothels in Saigon.

The Dismissal of General Nguyen Van Hinh

Following the arrest of two staff officers accused of conspiring against the Government, Ngo Dinh Diem suspended the Chief of Staff, General Nguyen Van Hinh, from his command on Sept. 11, 1954, and ordered him to leave for France. The general refused to obey or to lay down his command, and was supported by the sects, which issued a manifesto demanding the Government's resignation. On Sept. 22, however, the Caodaist and Hoa Hao leaders announced that they would support the Prime Minister if he formed a strong government in which they held a dominant position. Ngo Dinh Diem accordingly formed a coalition Government on Sept. 24 consisting of six Independents, three Caodaists, three Hoa Hao representatives, and five members of the Thin Thai (a cultural organization). He himself combined the Premiership with the portfolios of the Interior and Defence; Generals Nguyen Thanh Phuong and Tran Van Soai (the respective Caodaist and Hoa Hao commanders) became Ministers of State; and Dr. Tran Van Do (Thin Thai) retained the post of Foreign Minister.

The strained relations between the Government and the Army leaders gave rise during October and November 1954 to grave fears of a military coup and civil war. In view of this danger, General Collins (President Eisenhower's special representative in South Vietnam) gave warning on Nov. 17 that the Army would receive U.S. military aid only if it supported Ngo Dinh Diem. [This military aid had been promised to Ngo Dinh Diem's Government on Oct. 24, 1954.] General Nguyen Van Hinh left for Paris two days later to seek the support of Bao Dai; the latter, however, dismissed him from his post on Nov. 29, and the Prime Minister ordered that he should not be permitted to re-enter Vietnam. General Van Ty was appointed to succeed him on Dec. 8, 1954.

Political and Agrarian Reforms

General Trinh Minh Thé, the dissident Caodaist leader, rallied to the Government on Jan. 31, 1955, and the only serious military opposition encountered by the Government during January and February was from General Bacut's dissident Hoa Hao forces. The more peaceful conditions prevailing enabled the Government to introduce a number of measures for agrarian and political reform and for the suppression of corruption, the most important of which were the following:

(1) The establishment of a provisional and consultative National Assembly.

(2) A decree governing the level of rents for farm land.

(3) A decree declaring gambling to be illegal; this would weaken the financial position of the Binh Xuyen [see page 10].

Transfer of Military Command

An agreement transferring the command of all military forces in South Vietnam—except the French Expeditionary Corps—to the South Vietnamese Government, and terminating the financial assistance previously granted by the French Government to the armies of the sects, was signed on Feb. 10, 1955.

The Struggle with the United Front

The situation seriously deteriorated during March 1955, following the formation by the Caodaists, the Hoa Hao, the Binh Xuyen, and the Socialist Party on March 4 of a "United Front of Nationalist Forces". Its manifesto, which was signed by the leaders of the various groups and also by Generals Thé and Bacut, demanded the formation of a strong "Government of national unity," and stated that when such a Government had been formed they would merge their private forces in a single national army.

This demand was reiterated in an ultimatum presented to Ngo Dinh Diem by the United Front on March 21, 1955. On the same day they issued a press statement accusing him of totalitarianism, nepotism and suppression of freedom of the Press. Although the Prime Minister refused to compromise on the unification of all armed forces under a single command, and the abolition of the sects' privilege of levying taxes in the areas under their control, he offered on March 27 to replace those Ministers who were regarded as his personal followers. This proposal was followed by a split in the United Front, the Hoa Hao Ministers resigning from the Government on March 29, and several Independent and Thin Thai Ministers following their example during the next three weeks. General Thé, on the other hand, announced his support for Ngo Dinh Diem on March 27, as did the other Caodaist leaders on March 31, in return for a concession whereby the whole of the Caodaist forces (instead of only part of them, as had previously been envisaged) were incorporated in the Army.

Ngo Dinh Diem had meanwhile opened an attack on the Binh Xuyen on March 28 by transferring the command of the Saigon police to the Prefect of the city, and by sending troops to take over the city's police headquarters from the Binh Xuyen, who withdrew without resistance. During the night of March 29-30, however, fighting broke out between these troops and Binh Xuyen forces encamped nearby, 26 people being killed. As a counter-move to Ngo Dinh Diem's strategy, Saigon was blockaded from March 29 onwards by the Hoa Hao forces of Generals Soai and Bacut, and also by the Binh Xuyen forces.

On April 26, 1955, Ngo Dinh Diem again attacked the Binh Xuyen's control of the police by dismissing Lai Van Sang, director-general of the national security police. The Binh Xuyen refused to hand over the security headquarters building, and as a result a pitched battle between Government and Binh Xuyen troops raged over a large area of Saigon on April 28-29. After a desperate resistance the Binh Xuyen were expelled from most of their strongpoints in Saigon and Cholon, and withdrew to the marshy ground south and west of the city.

The Intervention of Bao Dai

On April 28, 1955, Bao Dai announced that he had transferred control of the armed forces from Ngo Dinh Diem to General Nguyen Van Vy (Inspector-General of the Army), who had fled to Dalat two days before and placed himself under the protection of the Imperial Guard. At the same time Bao Dai sent a message to Ngo Dinh Diem summoning him to Cannes for a conference of political and religious leaders, which he proposed should take place on May 5. To this message Ngo Dinh Diem replied on April 29 that the Cabinet regarded his presence in Saigon as indispensable, and also considered that General Vy should retain his present post. On April 30, in a telegram to the Prime Minister, Bao Dai accused him of being responsible for the bloodshed in Saigon, and repeated his order that he should go to Cannes. Bao Dai had previously announced on April 29 that he had ordered the former Chief of Staff,

13

General Hinh, to leave for Vietnam in order to discuss the problem of unification of the armed forces with the leaders of the United Front; General Hinh accordingly arrived by air at Pnom-Penh, the capital of Cambodia, on May 2.

Declaration of Bao Dai's Deposition made by the Revolutionary Committee

On April 29 General Vy arrived back in Saigon, and was promised support against Ngo Dinh Diem by General Le Van Ty (the Chief of Staff) and many other Army leaders. On April 20, however, a "Revolutionary Committee" led by the Caodaist generals Trinh Minh Thế and Nguyen Thanh Phuong, installed itself in the Prime Minister's palace, and on the same afternoon organized a "General Assembly of the Revolutionary Forces of the Nation" which met in the City Hall. This body declared Bao Dai deposed, and called on Ngo Dinh Diem to form a new provisional Government which would organize elections for a National Assembly and secure the withdrawal of the French Expeditionary Corps. During the evening Generals Vy and Ty went to the Prime Minister's palace, where they were arrested by the "Revolutionary Committee", forced to sign a document approving Bao Dai's deposition, and held prisoners until the Army compelled their release by threatening to storm the building.

Army Leaders Rally to Ngo Dinh Diem

On May 1 General Vy repudiated the statement which he had signed, and declared that Ngo Dinh Diem was "no longer a free agent". Shortly afterwards, however, General Ty again visited the Prime Minister's palace, where he met Ngo Dinh Diem and the Revolutionary Committee. As a result of their discussions, the Committee issued a statement declaring that it fully supported General Ty, and refusing to recognize any delegation of powers to Generals Vy and Hinh which might be ordered by Bao Dai. The officer corps rallied to the Prime Minister, and during the afternoon General Vy again fled to Dalat; he subsequently escaped to France, and on Jan. 13, 1956, was condemned to death *in absentia.*

General Ty's *volte-face* was variously attributed to the diplomacy of Ngo Dinh Diem, who played upon the professional rivalry between him and General Vy and promoted him to the rank of *général de division,* at the same time promoting a number of other officers, and to a message said to have been received during the morning of May 1, in which the U.S. Government was reported to have assured the Prime Minister of its continued support.

Meeting of States-General

Ngo Dinh Nhu (the Prime Minister's brother) announced on May 2 that a "States-General" composed of members of the provincial and municipal councils would meet on May 4 to depose Bao Dai and select a provisional Government. Later in the day, however, Ngo Dinh Diem met General Collins, who had just returned from a visit to Washington and was reported to have refused to give an assurance of continued U.S. support in the event of Bao Dai's deposition. Although this item was accordingly dropped from the agenda of the "States-General", the Prime Minister announced on May 3 his approval of a proposal by the Revolutionary Committee to summon, independently of the "States-General", an unofficial congress of "provincial revolutionary committees" to approve its resolution of April 30 [see above].

Opposing resolutions were adopted by the two factions in the "States-General" at its meeting on May 4-5. Government supporters from Tongking and Annam approved a Government-sponsored resolution calling on Bao Dai to hand over his powers to an elected National Assembly when it met; to restore his military powers to Ngo Dinh Diem; and to undertake not to dismiss him, to withdraw his full powers, or to interfere in the country's affairs. The Cochin-Chinese delegates, most of whom were opposed to both Bao Dai and Ngo Dinh Diem, called for the immediate formation of an "Assembly of the People", composed of provincial and municipal councillors, which would choose a provisional Government, control the elections to a National Assembly, and draw up a provisional Constitutional Charter defining the people's rights and liberties.

The Suppression of the Sects

The Government's troops (including Caodaist forces commanded by General Thé, who was killed in the fighting) renewed on May 2, 1955, their offensive against the Binh Xuyen, who abandoned their last post in Saigon during the night of May 9-10. Total casualties in the fighting since April 28 were given on May 22 as 215 killed and 1,500 wounded, including 60 civilians killed and 600 wounded. Although the main body of the Binh Xuyen linked up with Hoa Hao forces of Generals Bacut and Soai, about 1,500 Binh Xuyen troops continued to operate to the south of

15

Saigon, while during the summer Binh Xuyen agents conducted a terrorist campaign inside Saigon. On Sept. 21, 1955, Government troops launched an offensive against the Binh Xuyen headquarters in the Rungsat marshes (35 miles south of Saigon), as a result of which it was claimed that the rebels had been finally exterminated. The Binh Xuyen commander, General Le Van Vien, escaped and fled to France, and on Jan. 13, 1956, was sentenced by a military tribunal to death *in absentia.*

On the Hoa Hao side, General Bacut renewed his operations against the Government in the Sadec area (75 miles S.W. of Saigon) during the first week of May 1955, whilst General Soai, who had established his headquarters near Cantho (80 miles S.W. of Saigon), announced on May 13 his support for Bao Dai and his opposition to the Government. On May 27 the United Front's radio announced that General Hinh, whose whereabouts had remained obscure since his arrival in Pnom-Penh [see above], had taken command of the Hoa Hao and Binh Xuyen forces. Following a successful offensive by Government troops in the Cantho area during the fortnight June 5-18, however, General Hinh fled to Cambodia, whence he returned to Paris.

General Bacut had meanwhile withdrawn to the Cambodian frontier area, where he conducted a guerrilla campaign which tied down 50 to 80 battalions of the Government forces for the next nine months. The rebel forces were greatly weakened, however, by the surrender of General Soai on Feb. 19, 1956, with 4,700 of his men. On April 13, 1956, armed resistance to the Government was virtually brought to an end by the capture of General Bacut, who was sentenced to death by a civil court on June 11, 1956, for murder, pillage and arson. He appealed against the sentence to a court-martial, but was again condemned to death on July 4 after being found guilty of treason.

Relations between the Government and the Caodaists again deteriorated during the first two months of 1956. About 2,000 of the troops formerly commanded by General Thé revolted at the beginning of January, and on Feb. 19 Government troops occupied Tayninh, the Caodaist "capital." The leader of the sect, Pham Cong Tac, subsequently fled to Cambodia.

Proclamation of the Vietnamese Republic

The Ministry of the Interior announced on Oct. 6, 1955, that a referendum would be held on Oct. 23 to decide whether Bao Dai should be deposed. This decision was denounced by Bao Dai, who, in a Note on Oct. 13 to the French Government and the British, U.S., Soviet, and Indian Embassies in Paris, dissociated himself from Ngo Dinh Diem's policy.

A communiqué issued by Bao Dai's office in Paris on Oct. 18 announced that he had dismissed Ngo Dinh Diem from the Premiership and had annulled the full powers delegated to him. In a message to the Vietnamese people, published on the following day, Bao Dai explained that he had taken this action because "police methods and personal dictatorship must be brought to an end, and I can no longer continue to lend my name and my authority to a man who will drag you into ruin, famine and war".

The referendum held on Oct. 23 resulted in a 98 per cent majority against Bao Dai, the official results being as follows: for Bao Dai's deposition, 5,721,735; against, 63,017; spoiled votes, 44,105.

South Vietnam was officially proclaimed a republic, with Ngo Dinh Diem as its President, on Oct. 26, 1955. President Diem, who retained the posts of Prime Minister and Defence Minister, and assumed that of Supreme Commander of the Armed Forces, reappointed his previous Cabinet on Oct. 29, with two minor changes. The new regime was recognized on Oct. 26-27 by France, the U.S.A., Great Britain, Australia, New Zealand, Italy, Japan, Siam and South Korea, and on Dec. 12 by the Holy See.

Election of Constituent Assembly

The Government announced on Jan. 23, 1956, that general elections for a Constituent Assembly would be held on March 4. Under the electoral law, the Assembly was required to ratify a Constitution to be drafted by the President; if it failed to do so within 45 days it would be dissolved, and the Constitution would be submitted to a referendum. The Assembly

17

would be elected by all South Vietnamese citizens over 18 years of age, and would consist of 123 members, of whom 63 would represent Cochin China, 39 Annam, 12 the refugees from North Vietnam, and 9 the ethnic minorities of Annam. Candidates were required to be over 25, to have lived in South Vietnam for the six months preceding the elections, and to produce a "judicial certificate" establishing that they were not Communist or rebel sympathizers.

Before the elections a number of measures were taken against suspected opponents of the regime. It was announced on Jan. 11 that the "Revolutionary Committee" had been dissolved, and when this was denied by its president Nguyen Bao Toan, its headquarters were occupied by troops. Dr. Pham Quang Dan, leader of the Republican Party (a Caodaist organization), was arrested on Feb. 19 for distributing leaflets protesting against the electoral law; many alleged Communists (reported as about 8,000) were also arrested, and numerous Independent candidatures were suppressed. The Press censorship was temporarily lifted during the election campaign, but the publication of news or comment favouring "Communist or anti-national" activities remained punishable by six months' to five years' imprisonment. Most of the Opposition parties boycotted the elections in consequence, on the ground that no genuine freedom of speech or of the Press existed, although a number of Opposition candidates stood as Independents.

The voting, in which about 85 per cent of the electorate took part, passed off peacefully in most areas; in some country districts, however, polling stations were burned down, or grenades were thrown into them while voting was in progress. The results, issued on March 9, showed that at least 101 of the 123 members of the Assembly were expected to support the Government, the distribution of seats being as follows:

National Revolution Movement	66
Citizens' Rally	18
Workers' Party	10
Conquest of Liberty Party	7
Social Democrats	2
Dai Viet	1
Independents	19

Four pro-Government parties were represented in the Assembly: the National Revolution Movement, led by Tran Chanh Thanh (Minister of Information); the Citizens' Rally, a Roman Catholic organization led by Tran Van Lam; the Conquest of Liberty Party, led by Bui Van Thinh (Minister of the Interior); and the Workers' Party. The Social Democrats and the Dai Viet were the only Opposition parties represented.

The Assembly held its first session in Saigon on March 15. In a message to the Assembly, President Diem proposed on March 19 that it should itself draft the Constitution, which, he suggested, should be modelled on that of the United States. The period of 45 days granted to the Assembly in which to draw up a Constitution expired on April 29, but was subsequently extended on June 2 by another 30 days.

Adoption of New Constitution

The new Constitution of South Vietnam, which had been unanimously approved by the Constituent Assembly, was officially promulgated on July 7, 1956—the second anniversary of President Diem's accession to power.

The Constitution provided for a division of powers between the Executive, headed by the President, the Legislative Assembly, the members of which were excluded from public office, and the Judiciary, headed by a Constitutional Court. Both the President and the Assembly would be chosen by direct suffrage, the former for six years and the latter for four. Ngo Dinh Diem was declared to be the first President of the Republic and eligible for re-election, and was empowered to choose the first Vice-President, whilst it was provided that the Constituent Assembly should serve as the first Legislative Assembly. Legislation might be sponsored by either the President or the Assembly, and in the event of a serious disagreement between them the issue would be referred to a national referendum. When the Assembly was not in session the President might legislate by decree, subject to review when the Assembly convened. The President might veto laws passed by the Assembly, but a three-fourths majority of the Assembly might override his veto. Freedom of speech, of the Press, and of assembly were guaranteed, but during the next four years the President might suspend these rights by proclaiming a state of emergency.

Measures against Opposition Organizations

Armed opposition to the Government continued during the summer, several thousand Caodaist troops being reported in revolt during July and Binh Xuyen forces being active between Saigon and Dalat. Unrest was also reported in the trade union movement, in which connexion the Vietnamese Confederation of Christian Workers compelled the

19

Government early in July to release a number of arrested trade unionists by threatening to call a general strike.

Strong measures were adopted by the Government during July and August against the various sections of the Opposition. Le Van Thien, general secretary of the Socialist Party and a member of the "Revolutionary Committee", was arrested in July on a charge of having visited the dissident Caodaist zone to establish contact between the rebels and the Committee, which had adopted an attitude of open opposition to the Government. On Aug. 17 Lieutenant Nguyen Van Phuoc, an officer with a distinguished war record, was sentenced to death for entering the Binh Xuyen zone, and it was announced that 23 prominent political figures, including Nguyen Huu Than (a former vice-president of the Assembly of the French Union) and Tran Van An (formerly Minister of Information in General Van Xuan's Cabinet of 1948) would be tried by court-martial on a charge of participating in anti-Government activities during the spring of 1955. Colonel Nguyen Thanh Danh, a brother of the former Caodaist commander (General Nguyen Thanh Phuong), and general secretary of the Caodaist party *Vietnam Phuc Quoc Hoi*, was arrested on Aug. 20.

A decree signed by President Diem on Aug. 22 prescribed sentences of death or penal servitude for any Vietnamese or foreigner convicted of passing on to foreign Powers or Communist organizations information considered vital to national security.

Three-Power Talks on Vietnam

The political crisis of March-May 1955 brought to a head differences of opinion which had arisen between the French and U.S. Governments over their policies in South Vietnam. Whereas M. Faure, the then French Prime Minister, stated on April 29, 1955, that it had been evident for some time that Ngo Dinh Diem's Government was "not adapted to its mission", a U.S. State Department spokesman reaffirmed on the same day the U.S. Government's full support for Ngo Dinh Diem.

The differences between France and the U.S.A. were further aggravated following the appearance of the "Revolutionary Committee", which, French sources alleged, had been set up on U.S. advice to give the South Vietnamese Government a semblance of popular support. Deep offence was caused in France by the violent anti-French propaganda carried on by the South Vietnamese Government and the "Revolutionary Committee", and in particular by allegations–made by both South Vietnamese and U.S. official sources–that the French military authorities had assisted the Binh Xuyen. These charges were categorically denied on May 4 by both M. Faure and General Ely, the French Commissioner-General and C.-in-C. in South Vietnam.

In view of these differences, three-Power talks on the South Vietnamese question were held in Paris from May 7-12, 1955, between M. Faure, M. Pinay (then French Foreign Minister), Mr. Dulles (then U.S. Secretary of State), and Mr. Macmillan (then British Foreign Secretary). M. Faure stated on May 13 that a complete understanding had been reached; that neither France nor the U.S.A. intended to interfere in South Vietnam's internal affairs; and that both countries supported Ngo Dinh Diem's Government, though they wished to see it become more representative. M. Faure added that no official request had been received from South Vietnam for the withdrawal of the French Expeditionary Corps, but that a programme had been laid down for its repatriation.

Commenting on the Paris talks, Ngo Dinh Diem declared on May 14 that as a sovereign country South Vietnam could not be bound by decisions taken at conferences in which she was not a participant.

Relations between France and South Vietnam

Relations between the French and South Vietnamese Governments remained strained after the Paris talks despite M. Faure's pledge of support for Ngo Dinh Diem.

General Ely, whose repeated attempts at conciliation during the struggle between the Government and the sects had been strongly criticized by Ngo Dinh Diem, tendered his resignation on May 20, 1955, and left Saigon on June 2. The appointment of M. Henri Hoppenot, the permanent French representative on the U.N. Security Council, as his successor was announced on June 4, 1955.

Negotiations for the conclusion of military and cultural agreements, which opened in Paris on Aug. 14, 1955, remained deadlocked, as France was unable to accept certain South Vietnamese demands–notably that the Expeditionary Corps should be placed under Vietnamese command. The negotiations were accordingly broken off by South Vietnam on Oct. 13.

On Oct. 29, 1955, the South Vietnamese Government gave notice of termination of the general monetary and trade agreement with France concluded on Dec. 30,

1954, which provided for free monetary transfers between the two countries and granted preferential tariff treatment to French imports.

Evacuation of French Expeditionary Corps

The South Vietnamese Government informed the French Government at the end of January 1956 that it wished the French Expeditionary Corps to be withdrawn, in accordance with France's commitment under the Geneva Agreements to evacuate her troops from Indo-China when requested by the Governments concerned. The main body of the Expeditionary Corps was accordingly withdrawn by April 25, with the exception of 3,000 men entrusted with the liquidation of the French bases in South Vietnam—which, under an agreement concluded on March 22, was to be completed by June 30. The French High Command in South Vietnam was formally dissolved on April 28, when General Jacquot, the French C.-in-C., left Saigon for France.

The French Government accepted on July 21 a South Vietnamese request that the French High Commissioner's Office in Saigon should be transformed into an embassy; at the same time the South Vietnamese Government approved the nomination of M. Jean Payart as the first French Ambassador to South Vietnam. M. Hoppenot, the last French High Commissioner, had left Saigon a few days earlier.

II. THE ELECTIONS ISSUE

Failure to Reach Agreement on Elections throughout Vietnam
The final declaration of the Geneva Conference provided for consultations between North and South Vietnam in preparation for the holding of elections in July 1956. The Foreign Minister of North Vietnam (Pham Van Dong) stated on June 6, 1955, that his Government was prepared to open such consultations; at the same time he gave an assurance that North Vietnam desired free elections in which "all political parties, organizations, and individuals" would be able to take part.

Ngo Dinh Diem (then Prime Minister of South Vietnam) declared in a broadcast on July 6, 1955, however, that as the Geneva Agreements had not been signed South Vietnam was in no way bound by them; although it did not reject "the principle of elections" as a means of unifying the country, there could be no question of considering any proposals from the Vietminh "if proof is not given us that they put the higher interests of the national community above those of Communism"

In a Note of July 19, 1955, Pham Van Dong had asked Ngo Dinh Diem to nominate delegates to a pre-elections conference. The British, French, and U.S. diplomatic representatives in Saigon subsequently handed identical Notes to Ngo Dinh Diem on July 26 emphasizing their interest in seeing the Geneva Agreements respected, and urging him to open discussions with North Vietnam. Ngo Dinh Diem, however, rejected any

23

such talks, declaring on Aug. 10 that South Vietnam was "the only legal State", and reaffirming the policy laid down in his broadcast of July 6. On Sept. 21, 1955, he issued a second statement declaring that "there can be no question of a conference, even less of negotiations".

The situation remained deadlocked until the beginning of 1956 when, partly as a result of proposals made by the Premier of the Chinese People's Republic, Chou En-lai, and partly as a result of a British proposal, discussions were held in London from April 10 to May 8, 1956, between Lord Reading (Minister of State at the British Foreign Office) and Mr. Gromyko (Soviet Deputy Foreign Minister) on the question of the implementation of the elections clause of the Geneva Agreement. The two Governments, at the conclusion of the talks, expressed concern to the Vietnamese Governments that the provision of the Geneva Agreement for discussions between them on this subject had not been carried out, and appealed to them to agree on a date for such discussions.

The South Vietnamese Government, in its reply on May 25, 1956, reiterated its refusal to recognize the Geneva Agreements but promised not to "have recourse to solutions of violence", and to respect the demarcation line and the demilitarized zone. It declared that South Vietnam was in favour of free elections, but stated that "the absence of all liberties in North Vietnam makes impracticable at the moment any approach to the problem of electoral and pre-electoral operations". The North Vietnamese Government, on the other hand, offered on June 4 to open discussions with South Vietnam, and stated that it would ask for a new Geneva Conference if South Vietnam maintained its "negative attitude".

After an interval of nearly a year, the North Vietnamese Government renewed its demand for the implementation of the Geneva Agreements in the summer of 1957. In a letter to President Diem (July 18) Pham Van Dong suggested that discussions should take place on the organization of elections, and that postal services between the two zones should be restored as a step towards reunification. The South Vietnamese Government replied (in a communiqué issued on July 26) that it could "examine no proposal of the Vietminh Communists without proof and guarantee that they place the supreme interests of the nation above the interests of Communist imperialism", and that the subjection of the North to the

24

Communist system was a fundamental obstacle to reunification. The Northern Government nevertheless proposed on Sept. 25, 1957, the holding of a conference to consider the re-establishment and development of economic relations between the two zones—a proposal which met with no response.

In a letter to President Diem on March 7, 1958, Pham Van Dong repeated his proposal for a conference, which, he suggested, should meet at an early date to discuss a reduction in the number of troops on both sides and the establishment of trade relations with a view to promoting reunification; the letter strongly criticized "American interference in the internal affairs of South-East Asian countries", particularly Vietnam. In Saigon, the Northern offer was officially described as "phoney" and "a propaganda trick", and on April 26 the South Vietnamese Government issued a declaration rejecting it.

After stressing the "contradictions between the declarations and actions of the authorities in Hanoi", the statement said that the South Vietnamese Government also aimed at the country's reunification, general elections, free circulation between North and South, reduction of military forces, commercial exchanges and loyal relations. Before any negotiations could be considered, however, "authorities in Hanoi must prove their good faith" by meeting the following six conditions: (1) they should allow the 92,319 people who, it was claimed, wished to leave the Northern territory for South Vietnam to do so; (2) they should reduce their military forces to the level of those in the South; (3) they should renounce the use of "methods of terrorism and sabotage"; (4) they should allow the population of the North to "work in freedom and raise their living standards"; (5) they should cease "to force the population to conduct propaganda in their favour in letters sent to the South"; and (6) they should "establish democratic liberties similar to those existing in the South".

First Elections of National Assembly in South Vietnam

Although deadlock was reached in discussions on elections covering North and South Vietnam, general elections were held in South Vietnam in 1959, on Aug. 30. These resulted in an overwhelming victory for the Government, all but two of the 123 seats in the National Assembly being won by parties or Independent candidates supporting President Diem. The distribution of seats was as follows:

National Revolutionary Movement 78
Vietnamese Socialist Party 4
Social Democratic Party 3

Although greater freedom of speech was allowed than in the 1956 elections, Government officials maintained rigid control over every detail in order to prevent the infiltration of Viet Cong (Communist) elements; Western correspondents in Saigon pointed out that while this had been achieved, it had also led to the exclusion of a vigorous non-Communist Opposition. All the political parties permitted to take part in the elections consisted of Government supporters; the two Opposition members returned, Dr. Phan Quang Dan and Phan Khac Suu, stood as Independents because their party, the Democratic Bloc, had been refused registration.

Dr. Dan founded the Democratic Bloc in 1957 to press for greater civil liberties, whilst at the same time supporting the fight against the Communists with American aid, and advocating closer economic and cultural relations with France.

When the new Assembly met for the first time on Oct. 5, Dr. Dan and another Independent deputy, Nguyen Tran—both elected by large majorities in Saigon—were not permitted to attend, and the Ministry of State Security subsequently informed the Assembly's credentials committee that their election was invalid. Both had been found guilty and fined on Aug. 28 on charges of infractions of the electoral law, their appeals being rejected by the Court of Cassation on Sept. 15.

III. DIFFICULTIES OF THE DIEM REGIME — OPEN U.S. SUPPORT

Committee for Progress and Liberty

A "Committee for Progress and Liberty," formed early in 1960 with the aim of liberalizing the regime and permitting the emergence of a non-Communist political Opposition, consisted of eighteen members including nine former Ministers, doctors, lawyers, intellectuals and leading members of the Roman Catholic community and the Cao Dai and Hoa Hao sects. Dr. Tran Van Do (Foreign Minister in President Diem's first cabinet), Tran Van Van (a former Minister of National Economy) and Phan Khac Suu (a member of the National Assembly) were all members of the Committee.

On April 30, 1960, the Committee sent the President a petition, wherein the Government were accused of denying elementary civil liberties, of enforcing one-party rule and copying "Communist dictatorial methods", of silencing the Press and public opinion, and of carrying out widespread arrests which had "filled the gaols to overflowing". It was also alleged that the Government bureaucracy was paralysed by nepotism and corruption; that the Army had been weakened by making political affiliation more important than military efficiency; and that the country's economy was largely in the hands of speculators who were using the ruling party as a screen for their operations. To right these abuses, the President

27

was urged to take measures to liberalize the regime and to restore fundamental rights.

Tran Van Van, chairman of the "Committee for Progress and Liberty", emphasized that it was opposed to Communism but believed that "a regime without corruption, with more liberty and efficiency", would combat Communism more effectively than was being done.

Attempted Coup in Saigon

A number of Army officers led by Colonel Nguyen Chanh Thi attempted to carry out a *coup d'état* in Saigon in the early hours of Nov. 11, 1960, when parachute troops under their command occupied the General Staff and police headquarters, the airport, the general post office and the radio station, and besieged the presidential palace. The parachutists, who were joined by armoured troops and marines, tried to break into the strongly guarded presidential palace but abandoned the attempt after heavy fighting with loyalist troops. Apart from some student demonstrations, the civilian population remained passive, and during the afternoon of Nov. 11 General Le Van Ty (the Chief of Staff), who had been arrested at the beginning of the coup, was released by the rebels and began negotiations with them on the instructions of President Ngo Dinh Diem, who had been in the palace since the beginning of the uprising.

Later in the day, however, it was announced by Lieut.-Colonel Vuong Van Dong (Colonel Thi's second-in-command) and Dr. Phan Quang Dan (leader of the outlawed Free Democratic Party, who had been excluded from the National Assembly—see page 26) that a five-man Revolutionary Committee had been set up with Lieut.-Colonel Duong as chairman, Colonel Thi as vice-chairman, and Dr. Dan as one of its members; the names of the other two members were not given. The fact that Lieut.-Colonel Dong was named chairman of this committee, with precedence over his superior officer, confirmed reports that he, and not Colonel Thi, was the real leader of the attempted coup.

Rebel spokesmen stated that their aim was to establish "true democracy and liberty" in South Vietnam and to continue the fight against Communism. To this end the Revolutionary Committee would dismiss the National Assembly (the elections to which had been criticized by Opposition elements as "undemocratic") and hold

28

power until a new Assembly had been elected and a new Government formed; meanwhile freedom of the Press, assembly, and opinion would be proclaimed. The spokesmen claimed that the President had agreed to resign and that they were waiting for him to surrender and place himself under their protection.

Although the rebels had captured the radio station, broadcast appeals were made by President Diem—apparently from a transmitter in the palace—for military reinforcements to be sent to Saigon from the surrounding area. In response, armoured and infantry units entered the capital on Nov. 12 and moved on the presidential palace, from which the rebel parachutists withdrew to their barracks. The parachutists subsequently surrendered to the loyalist troops without resistance, but heavy fighting went on round the radio station before it was recaptured. According to official statements, over 300 people were killed and wounded during the 48-hour revolt, including 45 parachutists killed.

President Diem announced after the suppression of the revolt that its leaders would be brought to trial but that no action would be taken against the rank and file, who had been misled into action by being told that the presidential palace had been occupied by Communists, and who had ceased fighting immediately they realized the true situation; 15 rebel officers—who were believed to include Colonel Thi and Lieut.-Colonel Dong—had meanwhile succeeded in escaping by air to Cambodia, where they were interned. It was announced on March 2, 1961, that Dr. Dan, Tran Van Van and Phan Khac Suu would be tried by a military court on charges arising out of the attempted coup.

Administration Reforms

Within a few weeks of the abortive coup important administrative reforms were announced by President Diem on Feb. 6, 1961, designed to increase the efficiency of the administration. Details were as follows:

(1) A reduction from 20 to six in the number of agencies directly attached to the Presidency, the remainder being placed under appropriate Government departments.

(2) The creation of two new departments, each under a Minister—for Rural Affairs, to take over the Offices of Agricultural Development, Agricultural Credit and Rural Reconstruction; and for Civic Action, Information and Youth.

(3) The grouping of the Government departments dealing respectively with security, economic development and cultural and social affairs.

29

(4) The creation of a National Economic Council and a Cultural and Social Council to help in preparing Government projects and programmes, and of a Cultural Institute to help promote scientific research and artistic activities.

(5) As a first step towards fully elected village councils, a member responsible for youth and information work would be elected to each existing council by the local members of the Government's youth organization; elected village, municipal and provincial councils would subsequently be established.

National Economic Council

In the same month the National Assembly passed a Bill setting up the National Economic Council, comprising 45 representatives of agriculture, industry, commerce, transport, banking, fisheries, handicrafts and co-operatives (including 17 trade union representatives) and 10 economists. This body, officially inaugurated on Jan. 8, 1962, would give advice on all legislation relating to economic affairs and would be consulted on economic, financial, and social problems whenever the President considered it necessary.

Presidential Elections

Elections for the Presidency and Vice-Presidency, held on April 9, 1961, were contested by three pairs of candidates: (1) President Diem and Vice-President Nguyen Ngoc Tho; (2) Nguyen Dinh Quat and Nguyen Thanh Phuong; (3) Dr. Ho Nhut Tan and Nguyen The Truyen.

In his policy statements President Diem promised to increase the size of the Army and promote higher standards of efficiency and honesty in the Civil Service; a social insurance programme; heavier investment in industry; and expansion of the area under cultivation. He stated that Opposition parties would be allowed to function only within the concept of "national discipline".

The two Opposition candidates attacked President Diem's "family rule" and the Government's "arbitrary methods," and called for freedom of speech and of the Press, the release of all political prisoners, and measures against corruption; Nguyen Dinh Quat also called for a cease-fire with the Viet Cong rebels and nationwide elections with a view to the reunification of Vietnam. During the election campaign the heavily censored Press unanimously supported President Diem and strongly attacked the Opposition candidates.

The official results of the elections, in which about 85 per cent of the electorate voted, were:

President Diem	5,997,927
Nguyen Dinh Quat	268,668
Dr. Tan	475,125

The Opposition vote was largest in Saigon, where President Diem received less than half the potential vote in the capital; in the provincial constituencies, however, he obtained overwhelming majorities. Both the Opposition candidates alleged "terrorization" and "intimidation" by provincial officials against their supporters during the election campaign.

The four defeated candidates stated on May 24, 1961, that they had formed an organization called the Democratic Opposition Party, which they had asked the Government to register as a legal political party. Its aims were described as "the unification of Vietnam against dictatorship and Communism, and the reconstruction of the republic on the basis of democracy and civil liberties".

Cabinet Reorganization

An extensive governmental reorganization was carried out by President Diem on May 27, 1961, implementing at the same time the administrative reforms described above. The new Cabinet, all of whose members were designated Secretaries of State, included three Co-ordinating Secretaries ("super-Ministers"), as well as new Ministers for Rural Affairs and Civic Action.

Intensification of Communist Guerrilla Activities

From the end of 1959 onwards, and throughout 1960 and 1961, the Communist Viet Cong guerrillas intensified their activities on an ever-increasing scale in many parts of the country, notably in the Mekong delta, in the Point Camau area in the extreme south, and in the jungle areas along the Cambodian frontier. In nearly every month during 1960 and 1961 there were several hundred casualties in fighting between the guerrillas and Government forces, the latter being at a considerable disadvantage owing to the difficult nature of the terrain—e.g. in the Mekong delta, where high grass and mangrove swamps greatly facilitated guerrilla operations, and in the jungles of the hinterland. By the end of 1961 it was estimated that about 20,000 Viet Cong guerrillas were active in different parts of the country, against an estimated 6,000-7,000 a year earlier, necessitating a major military effort by the Government forces. According to foreign press correspondents in Saigon the Government had about 170,000 troops

31

on active service during the later months of 1961, although about four-fifths were needed to guard provincial administrations and were therefore virtually immobilized.

Proclamation of State of Emergency

President Diem proclaimed a state of emergency throughout South Vietnam on Oct. 19, 1961, when the National Assembly passed a Bill giving him powers for one year to issue all decrees necessary "to protect national security and mobilize manpower resources"; a fortnight earlier the President had told the National Assembly that South Vietnam was faced "no longer with a guerrilla war but with a real war waged by an enemy who ... is seeking a strategic decision in South-East Asia in conformity with the orders of the Comintern." The state of emergency was proclaimed on the same day that General Maxwell Taylor, special military adviser to President Kennedy, arrived in Saigon to assess what further support could be given to South Vietnam by the United States [see below].

Defence Policy for the Villages

With the aim of removing peasants in outlying areas from the influence of the Viet Cong, the Government adopted early in 1960 a policy of moving the peasantry from isolated villages to fortified settlements known as "agrovilles". Although the resettlement was in theory on a voluntary basis, many of the peasants were compelled to move to the agrovilles by the military authorities; in view of the strong opposition aroused, it was reported in April 1961 that the Government had decided not to set up more agrovilles when the establishment of the 26 originally planned was completed. Later in the year the Government began to organize a village "self-defence programme" whereby villages in outlying areas were protected by palisades, hidden traps and other tactical defence measures. At the same time the rural population were encouraged to hunt down Viet Cong guerrillas and agents who were operating in the countryside.

Mekong Flood Disaster

The Government's campaign against the Viet Cong was greatly hampered by a major flood disaster which inundated some 2,500 square miles in the Mekong delta in October 1961, left half a million people homeless, and destroyed the country's entire rice surplus for the coming year, estimated at 300,000 tons. In three provinces the peasantry lost practically all their pigs and poultry and 10 to 15 per cent of their buffaloes (the Vietnamese peasant's animal of all work), as well as large quantities of farm machinery. Reports from press correspondents said that the disaster—caused by the flooding of the Mekong River—had reduced about 1,000,000 peasants to "rock-bottom poverty". Large-scale relief aid was sent by the United States, France, Great Britain, Australia, New Zealand, Malaya, Japan, Western Germany and many other countries.

U.S. Economic and Military Aid to South Vietnam

The intensification of Communist guerrilla activities in South Vietnam caused increasing anxiety to the U.S. Administration and resulted in a marked acceleration in American economic and military assistance to that country from the middle of 1961 onwards. During the summer of 1961, agreements were drawn up between the United States and South Vietnam providing for American economic and military aid to the South Vietnamese Government.

General Maxwell D. Taylor, special military adviser to President Kennedy, visited South Vietnam from Oct. 19-25, 1961, to make an on-the-spot assessment of the situation for the U.S. President. During his visit he met President Diem; had conversations with senior Vietnamese and U.S. officers, including Lieut.-General Lionel C. McGarr, head of the U.S. Military Advisory Group; and visited areas where the Viet Cong had been particularly active. After General Taylor had left for Washington, President Kennedy sent a letter to President Diem on Oct. 26 stating that he was awaiting General Taylor's report "with great interest", following which he would be "in a better position to consider with you additional measures we might take to assist the Republic of Vietnam in its struggle against the Communist aggressors".

The White House disclosed on Dec. 15 that further correspondence had taken place between the U.S. and Vietnamese Presidents (the dates were not given). President Diem, who initiated this correspondence, had stressed that "if we lose this war, our people will be swallowed up in the Communist bloc", and had also referred to the serious economic consequences of the flood disaster. In reply, President Kennedy had assured President Diem that the U.S.A. would "promptly increase our assistance to your defence effort as well as help to relieve the destruction of the floods", adding that U.S. aid in South Vietnam's defence effort would no longer be necessary "if the Communist authorities in North Vietnam stop their effort to destroy the Republic of [South] Vietnam".

In a joint statement on Jan. 4, 1962, the U.S. and South Vietnamese Governments announced details of "a broad economic and social programme aimed at providing every Vietnamese with the means for improving his standard of living", representing "an intensification and expansion of efforts already made for the same purpose during the past few years". Simultaneously with this programme, "measures to strengthen South Vietnam's defence in the military field" were being taken pursuant to the exchange of letters between Presidents Kennedy and Diem. All these steps—economic, social and military—demonstrated "the desire of the U.S. and Vietnamese Governments to do their utmost to improve the protection and prosperity of the Vietnamese in the face of Communist guerrilla aggression and depredations directed and supported by the Communist regime in Hanoi".

South Vietnamese Austerity Programme

The South Vietnamese Government's austerity programme, which was mentioned in the U.S.-Vietnamese statement of Jan. 4, 1962, was contained in ten decree-laws signed by President Diem on Dec. 29, 1961. Aimed at the "entire reshaping" of the country's economic and financial structure, particularly in the fields of external trade, customs duties, and exchange control, they were in large part drafted by Dr. Vu Quoc Thuc, who had previously headed a Vietnamese group of experts which had carried out joint military and economic studies with an American group headed by Dr. Eugene A. Staley.

Vice-President Nguyen Ngoc Tho (who was concurrently Co-ordinating Secretary of State for Economic Development) explained that the reorganization had been under consideration for three years; he said that it was all the more necessary because "in order to put our economic development programme into effect we must make the best possible use of the substantially increased American aid".

Air Attack on Presidential Palace

Two fighter-bombers of the South Vietnamese Air Force attacked the presidential palace in Saigon in the early morning of Feb. 27, 1962, with rockets and machine-gun fire, the attack lasting for about 25 minutes. One wing of the palace was demolished and 16 palace officials wounded; President Ngo Dinh Diem and his entourage escaped unhurt.

International Control Commission's Report on Violation of Geneva Agreement by North and South Vietnam and the United States

In a special report signed on June 2, 1962, the Indian and Canadian members of the International Control Commission (I.C.C.) ruled that fundamental provisions of the Geneva Agreement had been violated both by North Vietnam, which had encouraged and supported hostile activities in South Vietnam, and by South Vietnam, which had received increased military aid from and concluded a *de facto* military alliance with the United States.

The report held that there was evidence to show that "armed and unarmed personnel, arms, munitions and other supplies have been sent from the zone in the North to the zone in the South with the object of supporting, organizing, and carrying out hostile activities, including armed attacks, directed against the armed forces and administration of the zone in the South", and that the North Vietnamese Army had "allowed the zone in the North to be used for inciting, encouraging and supporting hostile activities in the zone in the South, aimed at the overthrow of the Administration in the South". It also stated that "the Republic of Vietnam has violated Articles 16 and 17 of the Geneva Agreement in receiving increased military aid from the United States . . . . Although there may not be any formal military alliance between the United States of America and the Republic of Vietnam, the establishment of a U.S. Military Assistance Command in South Vietnam, as well as the introduction of a large number of U.S. military personnel beyond the stated strength of the MAAG (Military Assistance Advisory Group), amounts to a factual military alliance, which is prohibited under Article 19 of the Geneva Agreement."

Stating that it was being hampered in its role of maintaining peace in Vietnam "because of denial of co-operation by both parties" the Commission recommended the co-chairmen of the Geneva Conference to take remedial action to ensure that "the parties:

(*a*) respect the zone assigned to the other party;

(*b*) observe strictly the provisions of Articles 16, 17 and 19 of the Geneva Agreement in respect of the import of war material and the introduction of military personnel;

(*c*) commit no act and undertake no operation of a hostile nature against the other party;

(*d*) do not allow the zones assigned to them to adhere to any military alliance and to be used for the resumption of hostilities or to further an aggressive policy;

(*e*) co-operate with the International Commission in the fulfillment of its tasks of supervision and control of the implementation of the provisions of the Geneva Agreement. . . ."

A dissenting statement issued by the Polish delegation contended that the picture of the situation in the majority report "does not correspond with the real state of affairs" as "it places on the same level doubtful and legally unfounded allegations of one of the parties, on the one hand, and grave and undeniable violations of the Geneva Agreement sustained by records and findings of the International Commission on the other. . . ".

It went on: "The majority has ignored in its special report violation of Article 14(c) of the Geneva Agreement by the authorities of the Republic of Vietnam by persecutions of former resistance members, followed by the persecutions of all democratic elements, which is certainly one of the most important causes of the widespread movement against the Government of Vietnam which recently has taken various forms of dissatisfaction and struggle. . . . Another cause of this movement is the refusal of the Government of Vietnam to act towards the reunification of Vietnam as foreseen in the Geneva Agreement, in spite of the repeated proposals made by the Democratic Republic of Vietnam and efforts of the International Commission in the past towards facilitating negotiations by the parties. . . ."

IV. OVERTHROW OF NGO DINH DIEM'S GOVERNMENT AND OTHER EVENTS DURING 1963-64

Conflict between President Ngo Dinh Diem's Government and the Buddhist community led to a major political crisis in South Vietnam during the summer and autumn of 1963, culminating in the overthrow of the regime by a military coup on Nov. 1. A military junta seized power under the leadership of Lieut.-General Duong Van Minh, who, however, was himself overthrown by a second coup on Jan. 30, 1964, a new Government being formed by Major-General Nguyen Khanh.

The Hué Incident – President Diem's Religious Policy

On May 5, 1963, celebrations took place at Hué on the 25th anniversary of the ordination as a bishop of Mgr. Ngo Dinh Thuc, Archbishop of Hué and President Diem's eldest brother, Vatican flags being publicly flown. Thich Tinh Khiet, the head of the Vietnamese Buddhist community, was asked by Ngo Dinh Can (another brother of the President and virtual ruler of the Hué area) to send the Archbishop a telegram of congratulation, but refused to do so, fearing that such a gesture would be regarded as evidence of his approval of the Government's religious policy. ["Thich" is an honorific applied to Buddhist monks, equivalent to "the Reverend".]

37

The Government on May 7 forbade Buddhist flags to be flown on May 8, which is traditionally celebrated as the birthday of the Buddha, although the Vatican flags were still being displayed, and Radio Hué was ordered on May 8 not to broadcast the day's religious ceremonies. An orderly crowd of about 20,000 Buddhists, including many women and children, gathered outside the radio station to protest, whereupon the local military commander called out troops which threw tear-gas grenades and finally opened fire with machine-guns. Nine people were killed, seven of them children, and about 20 wounded.

The Government officially attributed the casualties to "Viet Cong terrorists", an explanation indignantly denied by the Buddhist authorities. Eyewitnesses of the shooting included three West German members of the staff of Hué University, who at the Buddhist authorities' request informed the foreign Press, the principal Western diplomatic missions, the U.N. Secretary-General, several foreign Chiefs of Staff, the World Buddhist Confederation and the Vatican. All three were expelled from the country some weeks later.

The shooting in Hué brought to a head a crisis in relations between the Government and the Buddhist community which had been developing for some years. Although Buddhists form at least 70 per cent of the population and Roman Catholics less than 10 per cent, the Government was dominated by Catholics, headed by President Diem himself and his family. In the armed forces, the police, the Civil Service, the universities and the trade unions Buddhists had largely been ousted from key positions and replaced by Roman Catholics, and particularly Catholics from Annam (the home of the Ngo family), whom the President regarded as more reliable politically.

The principal instrument of the Government's religious policy was a statute promulgated under French rule and intended to aid Catholic missions, which imposed upon Buddhism the status of a private organization and required the Buddhist clergy to obtain official permission for any public activity. Although President Diem had promised in 1955 to annul this statute the promise had never been carried out, and a large dossier submitted to the President and the National Assembly by the General Association of Vietnamese Buddhists in 1960, giving details of the ill-treatment to which Buddhists had allegedly been submitted in several areas, had produced no result.

The Buddhist clergy submitted the following demands to President Diem on May 15, 1963: (1) freedom to fly the Buddhist flag; (2) an equal legal status for Buddhism and Catholicism; (3) the ending of the "terrorizing" of Buddhists; (4) freedom for Buddhist worship and preaching; (5) compensation for the families of those killed on May 8 and the punishment of those responsible. According to an official report, President Diem in reply told them that they were "damn fools" to ask for religious freedom which was already guaranteed in the Constitution.

The situation deteriorated further after troops used gas grenades to break up a student demonstration in Hué on June 3, 1963; according to Buddhist sources 142 people were injured, some of them being blinded. Troops were flown to the city, martial law was imposed, and a curfew introduced. The Tu Dam pagoda (the most sacred Buddhist sanctuary in Indo-China), inside which many monks and students were fasting as a protest, was surrounded by barbed wire to prevent people from entering, and its water and electricity supplies were cut off.

Although the U.S. Embassy attempted to persuade President Diem to come to terms with the Buddhists, it was believed that he was encouraged in his intransigent attitude by his family, and especially by his brother Ngo Dinh Nhu and the latter's wife. On June 8 the Women's Solidarity Movement (the paramilitary women's organization led by Mme. Ngo Dinh Nhu) issued a violent statement suggesting that the Buddhists had been infiltrated by Communist agents; this allegation was categorically denied by the Buddhist leaders, who declared on June 12 that "we are determined to keep our struggle on a strictly religious level".

A compromise agreement between the Government and the Buddhist leaders was signed on June 16, 1963. This provided: (1) that the Government would compensate the families of those killed in the Hué incident and would set up a commission to determine who was responsible; (2) that Buddhist priests would be free to preach and would enjoy the same rights as the Christian clergy; (3) that arrests and ill-treatment of Buddhists would end and those in custody be released; (4) that Buddhists might fly their religious flag if the national flag was flown

39

at the same time; (5) that the National Assembly would study the statute declaring Buddhism a private organization.

This agreement, which was reported to have been reached under pressure from the U.S. Government, satisfied neither side; many Buddhists resented in particular the Government's refusal to admit responsibility for the Hué incident, whilst Ngo Dinh Nhu and his wife disliked the concessions made by the Government. *The Times of Vietnam* (a Government-controlled English-language newspaper) repeated on June 17 the allegation that some Buddhist leaders had Communist associations, and on June 26 Ngo Dinh Nhu ordered the Republican Youth to agitate for the repudiation of the agreement.

A few hours after the signing of the agreement on June 16, the police clashed with a crowd who wished to take part in the funeral ceremonies for Thich Quang Duc — a 73-year-old Buddhist monk, who had burned himself to death in a public square in Saigon. A boy was said to have been shot dead by the police and many people injured, including 30 policemen. Although the Buddhist leaders demanded the release of those arrested in connexion with the riot as a sign of the Government's good faith in carrying out the agreement, it was announced on June 22 that 10 of the rioters would be tried on charges of assaulting the police.

Vice-President Nguyen Ngoc Tho announced on July 12 that the inquiry commission had confirmed that the Viet Cong was responsible for the deaths of those killed on May 8. This statement and the continued attacks on the Buddhists by *The Times of Vietnam* were believed to have been largely responsible for a change in the leadership of the Buddhist movement, which increasingly passed into the hands of the younger clergy, headed by Thich Tri Quang (41), a monk of North Vietnamese origin who had twice been arrested by the French on suspicion of co-operating with the Vietminh.

Trial of Leaders of 1960 Coup
Apparently as a warning to the Buddhist leaders and to their supporters in the armed forces, 19 soldiers and 34 civilians, including a number of prominent political figures, were tried by a military court during the first half of July 1963 on charges of supporting the attempted coup of Nov. 11, 1960, after nearly three years in prison. Thirteen soldiers were sentenced to prison terms of up to 18 years on July 8, the remaining six being

40

acquitted, whilst nine officers who had escaped to Cambodia were condemned to death *in absentia* on July 12. During the trial the prosecution alleged that two U.S. Embassy officials had been involved in the coup, a strong denial being issued by the Embassy; *The New York Times* commented that "the attempt to involve Americans is seen as a warning to them to stay out of any future attempted coups".

Phan Khac Suu (a former Opposition deputy) was sentenced to eight years' imprisonment on July 11, Dr. Phan Quang Dan (leader of the banned Free Democratic Party) to seven years, three other civilians to six years, and 15 to five years; 14 of the accused civilians were acquitted, including Dr. Tran Van Do (an uncle of Mme. Ngo Dinh Nhu and Foreign Minister in President Diem's first Government). Another of the accused, Nguyen Tuong Tam, had previously committed suicide on July 7 by taking poison.

Renewal of Buddhist Agitation

In a letter to President Diem, Thich Tinh Khiet accused the Government on July 15, 1963, of failing to carry out the agreement of June 16, and announced that the Buddhists would launch a new protest campaign. In Saigon police armed with clubs beat up monks and nuns who were sitting on the ground in a protest demonstration on July 17, arrested about 200 of them, and sealed off all the pagodas with barbed wire, allowing no one to enter or leave.

President Diem announced on July 18 that he had ordered all civil and military authorities to implement the agreement of June 16 and had given instructions that the use of the Buddhist flag should be permitted. The arrested monks and nuns were released on July 20 and the barricades round the pagodas removed. These conciliatory gestures were regarded as inadequate by the Buddhist leaders, who demanded that the Government should admit its responsibility for the Hué incident and release the Buddhist laymen still in prison, but both sides attempted to avoid a serious clash. Mass demonstrations in Saigon, Hué, Dalat and Nhatrang on July 30 passed off peacefully, the police making no attempt to intervene. The situation gravely deteriorated in the first week of August, however, as a result of violent statements made by Ngo Dinh Nhu and his wife.

Ritual Suicides by Buddhists

Feelings were further inflamed and the crisis intensified by a series of ritual suicides by Buddhists. A 21-year-old monk burned himself to death at Phan Thiet on Aug. 4; a 17-year-old novice at Hué on Aug. 13; a nun in a village near Nhatrang on Aug. 15; and a 71-year-old monk in the courtyard of the Tu Dam pagoda at Hué on Aug. 16. Of these, only the last suicide had been approved by the Buddhist authorities, the other victims acting on their own initiative. In Saigon an 18-year-old girl tried to cut off her left hand with a hatchet as an offering to the Buddha in the Xa Loi pagoda on Aug. 12. The suicides created a tense situation in both Saigon and Hué, where 47 members of the University staff resigned on Aug. 17 as a protest against the dismissal of the Catholic rector because he had not prevented students from taking part in demonstrations.

Mass Arrests of Buddhists

During the early hours of Aug. 21, 1963, the Special Forces and the police raided the principal pagodas in Saigon, Hué, Quangtri, Quangnam and Nhatrang. In Saigon hundreds of heavily-armed troops and police stormed the Xa Loi pagoda, arrested over 300 monks and nuns, and sacked the building; three other pagodas in the capital were also raided. In Hué the monks used drums and gongs to summon the population, who fought the troops with sticks and stones for eight hours; about 30 monks and nuns were reported to have been killed and 70 wounded during the storming of the Tu Dam pagoda, which was destroyed by an explosion.

State of Siege Declared

A proclamation was issued by President Diem at 6 a.m. on Aug. 21 declaring a state of siege throughout the country and empowering the Army to search houses at any time, to arrest all persons whose activities were considered harmful to public security, to forbid all gatherings likely to endanger public order, to restrict press freedom and control broadcasting, films and plays, and to prohibit the possession and circulation of all documents harmful to public order. All infringements of public security were to be tried by military courts. Brigadier-General Ton That Dinh was appointed military governor of Saigon, and General Tran Van Don Chief of Staff, in place of General Le Van Ty, who was seriously ill.

Resignation of Vu Van Mau, Tran Van Chuong and Mme. Tran Van Chuong

The Foreign Minister, Vu Van Mau, resigned on Aug. 22, shaved his head like a Buddhist monk, and asked for permission to make a pilgrimage to India. President Diem refused to accept his resignation, but granted him three months' leave in which to make his pilgrimage. Tran Van Chuong and his wife (the parents of Mme. Ngo Dinh Nhu) also resigned their respective posts as Ambassador in Washington and permanent observer at the U.N. on Aug. 22, their example being followed by all but two of the diplomatic staff of the Washington Embassy during the next four days. Do Vang Ly (Consul-General in India) was appointed Ambassador in Washington on Sept. 30.

Committee for the Defence of Pure Buddhism

This pro-Government Buddhist organization was formed on Aug. 23 under the leadership of a monk named Thich Thien Hoa, who declared that he entirely approved the raids on the pagodas and the arrests of monks as "indispensable for the protection of the country". In a letter to President Diem which was published on Aug. 26, Thich Tinh Khiet, who was detained in a military hospital, stated that he had authorized Thich Thien Hoa and three of his followers to negotiate with the Government in an attempt to find a peaceful solution. The pagodas occupied by the police were handed over to Thich Thien Hoa's committee on Aug. 31, but were boycotted by the mass of Buddhists and remained almost deserted.

Student Protest Movement

Following the mass arrests of Buddhist monks, the leadership of the protest movement passed to the students. Demonstrations began in Saigon on Aug. 23, and on the following day General Ton That Dinh closed the University and all schools in the capital; some 1,380 students were arrested on Aug. 25, and a girl was reported to have been killed and several other people wounded when the police opened fire to disperse demonstrators.

After the publication of Thich Tinh Khiet's letter (see above) the Government took a number of measures designed to conciliate Buddhist opinion. The curfew was lifted in Saigon on Aug. 28, most of the arrested students were released, and some of the troops brought into the capital were withdrawn to the outskirts. The schools were gradually reopened from Aug. 30; and the state of siege and the censorship lifted on Sept. 16; Thich Tinh Khiet was released three days later, and 107 of the Buddhists arrested in Hué on Oct. 2.

Unrest nevertheless continued, especially among the students, who from Sept. 7-12 staged widespread demonstrations against the Government; the schools were thereupon occupied by the police on Sept. 9 and nearly 3,000 students and schoolchildren arrested. From Saigon the agitation spread on Sept. 14 to Hué, Dalat, Bien Hoa, Nhatrang and Vinhlong, where hundreds more students were arrested. Following the circulation of leaflets calling on students to strike and demonstrate when the schools were reopened, further mass arrests of students were reported to have taken place on Oct. 19.

General Elections

Elections to the National Assembly took place on Sept. 27. An amendment to the Constitution had been adopted on July 8, 1962, shortly before the previous Assembly's original mandate was due to expire, extending the period between elections from three to four years. Voting had been fixed for Aug. 31, 1963, but was postponed on Aug. 27 because of the religious crisis. Although it was officially claimed that 6,329,831 electors out of 6,809,078 had voted, foreign correspondents reported that the elections had aroused little interest; some seats were contested, but all the candidates were Government supporters and had been approved by the Government in advance. The successful candidates included Ngo Dinh Nhu and his wife, who according to official figures received 99.9 and 99.8 per cent of the votes in their respective constituencies.

The new Assembly met on Oct. 7. In his opening speech President Diem denounced the U.N. General Assembly for discussing the Buddhist question in South Vietnam, which, he claimed, was "already settled".

U.S. Reaction to Religious Crisis

The U.S. State Department issued the following statement on Aug. 21 after the storming of the pagodas: "On the basis of information from Saigon it appears that the Government of the Republic of Vietnam has instituted severe repressive measures against the Vietnamese Buddhist leaders. These actions represent a direct violation by the Vietnamese Government of assurances that it was pursuing a policy of reconciliation with the Buddhists. The Unites States deplores repressive actions of this nature."

44

Mr. Robert S. McNamara (then U.S. Defence Secretary) and General Maxwell D. Taylor (chairman of the Joint Chiefs of Staff) visited South Vietnam from Sept. 24-Oct. 1, 1963, to assess the impact of the religious crisis on the war effort against the Viet Cong. A White House statement (Oct. 2) said that "Secretary McNamara and General Taylor reported their judgment that the major part of the U.S. military task can be completed by the end of 1965. . . . The political situation in South Vietnam remains deeply serious. The United States has made clear its continuing opposition to any repressive actions in South Vietnam. While such actions have not yet significantly affected the military effort, they could do so in the future. . . ."

A State Department spokesman refused on Oct. 8 to comment on reports that U.S. economic aid to South Vietnam had been suspended since late August, merely stating that the whole question of U.S. aid to South Vietnam was under close and continuous review. Senator Frank Church (Democrat) and 14 other Senators had previously put down a motion on Sept. 12 calling for the withdrawal of U.S. aid unless the South Vietnamese Government abandoned its repressive policies. It was reported on Oct. 22 that President Diem had been informed that the United States would not finance the Special Forces unless they were placed under the General Staff's command and transferred to field operations; they were accordingly withdrawn from Saigon on Oct. 30—a development which greatly facilitated the subsequent coup.

Military Coup in Saigon – Assassination of President Ngo Dinh Diem

The coup was launched shortly after noon on Nov. 1, when troops and marines occupied the Army and Navy headquarters, the arsenal, the radio station, the telegraph office, the police headquarters and other key points; at the same time senior officers regarded as supporters of the regime were arrested, among them Colonel Le Quang Tung (commander of the Special Forces), who was subsequently executed. Soon afterwards Saigon Radio broadcast an announcement that a Military Revolutionary Committee headed by Lieut.-General Duong Van Minh (chief military adviser to the President) was leading the revolt.

The main opposition to the coup came from the Presidential Guard and a section of the Navy. Aircraft machine-gunned warships in the port which

45

had remained loyal, and after some resistance the Navy rallied to the rebels. The barracks of the Presidential Guard were captured during the evening after being bombarded by tanks and artillery. The heaviest fighting occurred round the Presidential Palace, which was shelled throughout the night and finally taken by storm in the early hours of Nov. 2.

Admiral Harry Felt (U.S. C.-in-C., Pacific, who was visiting Saigon) and Mr. Lodge had been received by President Diem during the morning of Nov. 1, shortly before the coup began; according to unofficial reports from Saigon they unsuccessfully attempted to persuade him to resign, promising that his safety would be guaranteed, and several times during the afternoon telephone calls from the U.S. Embassy repeated this promise. The U.S. Government, however, repeatedly denied that it had been involved in the coup or had received any advance warning of it.

President Diem and Ngo Dinh Nhu escaped from the Presidential Palace before it was occupied by the insurgents; they were variously reported to have done so through a secret passage or in a car or ambulance. Arrested a few hours later in a Catholic church in Cholon (the Chinese suburb of Saigon), they were shot in a car while being taken to Army headquarters. First reports by Saigon Radio attributed their deaths to suicide, but on Nov. 6 it was officially stated that they had committed "accidental suicide" when Ngo Dinh Nhu tried to seize a pistol from the officer guarding them.

In Saigon mass demonstrations in support of the coup on Nov. 2-3 threatened to develop into riots. The homes of unpopular Ministers, deputies, and officials, the offices of pro-Government newspapers, and shops owned by Mgr. Ngo Dinh Thuc were sacked, and in some cases set on fire. The statues of the Trung sisters (legendary Vietnamese heroines), which were portraits of Mme. Ngo Dinh Nhu and her eldest daughter, were decapitated by artillery, while crowds danced the twist, the tango, and other dances banned under her legislation. The demonstrations never took an anti-Catholic form, however—largely, it was believed, because of the active part played by Catholic students in the opposition to President Diem's regime.

Hundreds of monks, students and other political prisoners were freed immediately after the coup, among them the Air Force lieutenant who had

46

machine-gunned President Ngo's palace in 1962, and who was promoted to captain on being released. Buddhist monks and laymen told the Press that while in prison they had been beaten, whipped, cut with knives and tortured by means of electric shocks or by having their heads held under water, and that at least one student had been beaten to death. The 33 prisoners condemned for taking part in the 1960 coup were released from the prison island of Poulo-Condor and brought on Nov. 7 to Saigon, where they were welcomed by enthusiastic crowds. A decree of Dec. 27 granted a general amnesty to all political prisoners, except those convicted of helping the Communists.

The National Revolutionary Movement, the Revolutionary Labour Party and the Women's Solidarity Movement were banned on Nov. 13. It was officially stated on Dec. 9 that 137 people had been arrested since the coup, and that 13 high officials of the former regime, including Duong Van Hieu (head of the secret police) would be tried on charges of corruption and abuse of their powers.

Religious Developments Following the Coup

At the conclusion of a four-day conference, the 11 principal Buddhist sects in South Vietnam agreed on Jan. 3, 1964, to unite in a single Buddhist Church. This organization would have two governing bodies—the Institute for Religious Affairs, the chairman of which would be the religious leader of all South Vietnamese Buddhists, and the Institute for Secular Affairs, which would deal with political and social questions.

Four people were killed and 18 wounded in fighting between Buddhists and Catholics in Binh Tuy province (60 miles north-east of Saigon) on Jan. 1. The Ministry of Security gave warning on Jan. 7 that persons responsible for attacks on Christians and Christian churches would be tried by a military court, and in grave cases might be sentenced to death.

Adoption of Provisional Constitution

The Military Revolutionary Committee suspended the Constitution on Nov. 4, 1963, pending its revision, and adopted a Provisional Constitution with the following clauses:

(1) South Vietnam would remain a republic.
(2) Legislative and executive powers were transferred to the Military Revolutionary Committee. [The National Assembly had already been dissolved on Nov. 2.]
(3) The chairman of the Committee (Major-General Duong Van Minh) would exercise the powers of Chief of State.
(4) The executive power was delegated by the Committee to a provisional

47

Government. The Committee would appoint a Prime Minister, who would choose his Ministers with the Committee's approval.

(5) The legislative power was also delegated to the provisional Government, with the exception of matters relating to the Budget, fiscal legislation, defence and security.

(6) Existing laws and regulations would temporarily remain in force, with the exception of those "contrary to the spirit of the November 1 revolution".

Policies of Provisional Government and Military Committee

The Provisional Government, formed by Nguyen Ngoc Tho (the former Vice-President) on Nov. 4, announced on the same day that it would lay the foundations of a truly democratic regime; continue the fight against the Viet Cong until victory was achieved; guarantee fundamental liberties; observe all South Vietnam's existing agreements; and strive to strengthen its links with friendly countries and to improve relations with neighbouring States. The Military Committee stated on the same day that its policy was one of "democracy within discipline" and that it would transfer power to a popularly elected Government "when the situation permits"; it guaranteed freedom of the Press and religion, and freedom for non-Communist parties to operate within the framework of national security.

The Military Committee formed on Nov. 6 a Central Executive Committee of 12 generals, which would be responsible for all major decisions until civilian rule was re-established; General Duong Van Minh was chairman of this body, Generals Tran Van Don (Defence Minister) and Ton That Dinh (Security Minister) first and second vice-chairmen, and General Le Van Kim general secretary. It was announced on the same day that a "Council of Sages" representing all nationalist bodies and the professional classes would be set up to advise the Government on fundamental questions. The Council—renamed the Council of Notabilities, and consisting of 60 members nominated by General Duong—met for the first time on Jan. 2, 1964.

Changes in Military Command and Cabinet

Changes in military and political appointments were announced on Jan. 5, 1964, as follows: (1) General Duong Van Minh was proclaimed supreme commander of the armed forces; (2) General Tran Van Don became C.-in-C.; (3) General Le Van Kim succeeded General Tran Van Don as Chief of Staff; (4) General Ton That Dinh was appointed head of the

48

Ministry of the Interior, which was re-established in place of the Ministry of Security; (5) Major-General Tran Thien Khiem succeeded General Ton That Dinh as commander of the 3rd Corps; (6) Brigadier-General Do Mau, previously head of military security, succeeded General Tran Tu Oai as Minister of Information; (7) three Deputy Chiefs of Staff were appointed, among them General Nguyen Van Vy.

The effect of these changes was to reduce the influence of General Ton That Dinh, by depriving him of the command of the Saigon area, and to concentrate power in the hands of the "triumvirate" of Generals Duong Van Minh, Tran Van Don, and Le Van Kim. General Nguyen Van Vy had, after his unsuccessful attempt in 1955 to overthrow the Diem Government [see pages 12-14] escaped to France, where he served as a colonel in the French Army, but returned to Vietnam in December 1063 at General Duong's invitation.

New Military Coup in Saigon

General Duong's regime was overthrown in the early hours of Jan. 30, 1964, by a bloodless military coup led by Generals Nguyen Khanh (Commander of the 4th Corps, in the Mekong delta) and Tran Thien Khiem. Tanks and parachutists took up key positions in the capital, General Duong's residence was placed under armed guard, and Generals Tran Van Don, Le Van Kim and Ton That Dinh were arrested, together with Major-General Mau Huu Xuan (prefect of Saigon and director-general of police). During the afternoon a meeting of 53 members of the Military Revolutionary Committee dissolved the Central Executive Committee and elected General Nguyen Khanh as chairman of the Military Committee in place of General Duong. A few minutes later General Nguyen Khanh broadcast a declaration alleging that "a number of persons seeking their own private interests have not hesitated to ally themselves with the colonialists and to advocate neutralization, thus paving the way for the Communists to enslave our nation." The Council of Notabilities approved on the same day a resolution calling on General Nguyen Khanh to break off diplomatic relations with France.

During the morning of Jan. 30 General Nguyen Khanh had a meeting with Mr. Lodge, at which he was reported to have stated that the object of the coup was to frustrate a plot by the arrested generals to impose a neutralist policy on South Vietnam with French support. The *Times* correspondent in Washington reported on Feb. 23 that "it is now admitted that the Ambassador, Mr. Henry Cabot Lodge, knew of the plans for the second coup at least 48 hours before it took place. . . ."

It was announced on Feb. 8, 1964, that General Duong Van Minh had agreed to remain Chief of State; an amendment to the Provisional Constitution adopted on the previous day provided that either the chairman of the Military Revolutionary Committee or a person appointed by that body would exercise the powers of Chief of State.

A new Government was formed on Feb. 8 with General Nguyen Khanh as Prime Minister and General Tran Thien Khiem as Defence Minister. The former loyalty of these two generals to President Diem, which was emphasized in broadcasts from North Vietnam, gave rise to fears that they intended to restore the Diem regime; the officer believed to have shot President Diem and Ngo Dinh Nhu committed suicide on Jan. 31. Apparently in order to allay these fears, the Government released on Feb. 6 seven prominent opponents of President Diem's regime who had been imprisoned since 1955, including Tran Van An (a former Minister of Information) and Nguyen Huu Thuan (Foreign Minister in M. Tran Van Huu's Government of 1948). A decree of Feb. 28 established a Revolutionary Court to try officials or prominent supporters of the Diem regime on charges of murder, torture, rape, illegal detention, corruption and activities detrimental to the national economy. The court, consisting of both civil and military judges, was empowered to pass the death sentence; those convicted would have no right of appeal, but if condemned to death might appeal for clemency.

Executive Committee Appointed

The Military Committee elected on March 22 a new Executive Committee consisting of General Nguyen Khanh (chairman), General Duong Van Minh ("supreme adviser" to General Nguyen Khanh), General Tran Thien Khiem, General Do Mau and Major-General Pham Xuan Chieu (vice-chairmen), and Brigadier-General Nguyen Van Thieu (general secretary). It was suggested in the foreign Press that the formation of this
50

body was intended to demonstrate the armed forces' support for General Nguyen Khanh, whose policy had been increasingly the subject of criticism.

General Elections to Be Held

The Council of Notabilities refused on March 31 a request by General Nguyen Khanh that it should dissolve itself. The Government thereupon announced on April 5 that the Council would be dissolved, and that general elections to a National Assembly would be held within four to six months, "depending on the degree of security in the country".

Deterioration in Relations with France

Relations between South Vietnam and France became extremely strained during January 1964 as a result of the French Government's support for the neutralization of Vietnam, as part of a general policy of neutralization in South-East Asia, and its decision to recognize the Chinese Communist Government. Students organized a series of anti-French demonstrations in Saigon during Jan. 13-17, and the Council of Notabilities adopted on Jan. 22 a resolution demanding the suspension of diplomatic relations. The Foreign Minister, Pham Dang Lam, informed the French Chargé d'Affaires on Jan. 24 that the Government had refused to accept the proposed new French Ambassador to South Vietnam, M. Robert du Gardier, who had served in the former French Administration in Indo-China, and on Jan. 28 an embargo was imposed on French imports.

A statement by the Provisional Government on Jan. 27 strongly protested against the French decision to recognize the Chinese Communist Government. "Communist North Vietnam", it declared, "has been able to wage and sustain its aggression against South Vietnam only thanks to the active support of the People's Republic of China, which continues to give it an ever greater military and technical assistance. . . . In extending formal recognition to the Peking regime, enemy of the Vietnamese people, France contributes, whether deliberately or not, to reinforcing the position of Communist China to the detriment of the free world, and to encouraging the expansion of Chinese Communism in this area of the world. . . ."

General Nguyen Khanh's Allegations of French Plot

General Nguyen Khanh asserted on Feb. 27 that French agents had hired a terrorist to assassinate him, and in subsequent statements alleged that they had put a price of 300,000,000 piastres (about £1,400,000) on his head, were plotting with the Communists to overthrow the Government and neutralize South Vietnam, and had taken part in an anti-American terrorist campaign in Saigon. [This campaign had intensified during February 1964, several Americans being killed.] The French Chargé d'Affaires strongly protested to Dr. Phan Huy Quat on March 2 against the publication of these allegations in Saigon newspapers.

The U.S. Secretary of State, Mr. Dean Rusk, said on March 6 that he had no evidence that France had been plotting against the South Vietnamese Government or had sought deliberately to undermine its war effort.

Anti-French Demonstrations

On July 19 (the tenth anniversary of the Geneva Agreements), which was observed as a "national day of shame", General Nguyen Khanh violently attacked the French Government's neutralization policy before a crowd of 40,000 people in Saigon; students afterwards burnt an effigy of President de Gaulle and daubed the French war memorial with paint. In the early morning of July 21 about 200 students broke into the French Embassy, the police making no attempt to intervene, smashed furniture and equipment, and set fire to a car. After the French Chargé d'Affaires had protested, the South Vietnamese Government apologized on July 25 and promised compensation. On July 29, however, students again attacked the war memorial, which was then demolished by soldiers; a second French protest was rejected by the Government on the ground that the memorial was the property of the Saigon prefecture, which was free to "preserve, modify or transform it".

V. THE CRISIS OF AUGUST – NOVEMBER, 1964

Disagreements between General Nguyen Khanh and Dai Viet Party

The minister of the Interior, Ha Thuc Ky, resigned on April 4 after General Nguyen Khanh had deprived him of the right to nominate provincial governors and high officials; Brigadier-General Lam Van Phat (a Catholic and a former supporter of President Ngo Dinh Diem) was appointed to succeed him on April 7. Ha Thuc Ky's resignation was the first indication of a growing split between General Nguyen and the Dai Viet Party, which held several key posts in his Government.

The *Dai Viet Quoc Dan Dang* (Nationalist Party of Greater Vietnam), a right-wing party with an authoritarian philosophy formed in 1941, collaborated successively with the Japanese, the Vietminh, and the Bao Dai regime, but was driven underground by President Ngo Dinh Diem, although its policy had much in common with his own. It supported General Nguyen Khanh's coup of Jan. 30, 1964, and formed the strongest political group represented in his Government; General Nguyen Khanh, however, was reported to have been alienated by its attempts to secure a monopoly of political power, and by the formation of a strong bloc of Dai Viet officers in the Army.

Growing Tension between Buddhists and Catholics

The most striking feature of the political situation during the spring and early summer of 1964 was the growing political activity of the Buddhists, which in turn led to great uneasiness among the Roman Catholic minority.

The Buddhist Press adopted an increasingly hostile attitude towards the Government and put forward demands for the recognition of Buddhism as the national religion. Several hundred thousand people took part in a demonstration in Saigon on May 26 to celebrate the Buddhists' resistance to President Diem's regime, the heart of Thich Quang Duc [the monk who had burned himself to death on June 11, 1963—see page 40] being carried in procession as a holy relic.

Apparently as a concession to Buddhist pressure, several persons accused of abuses of power under President Diem's regime were·brought to trial in June. Major Dang Sy, a Catholic officer who had ordered troops to fire on Buddhist demonstrators at Hue on May 8, 1963 [see page 38], was sentenced to life imprisonment on June 6, and other officials were sentenced to varying lengths of imprisonment.

To express their uneasiness following the trial of Major Dang Sy, 100,000 Roman Catholics demonstrated in Saigon on June 7 to protest against alleged religious discrimination against Catholics. In a letter to General Nguyen Khanh published on June 18, the Archbishop of Saigon (Mgr. Nguyen Van Binh) alleged that Catholics were being "unjustly accused and ill-treated" and defended Major Dang Sy, who, he declared, had "loyally done his duty" on May 8, 1963.

Adoption of New Constitution

General Nguyen Khanh proclaimed a state of emergency on Aug. 7, declaring that the country was facing "a Communist army on our territory of 150,000 men, of whom 34,000 are regulars," and pressure from North Vietnam on the 17th parallel, whilst Chinese troops were massed on the southern frontier of China and stationed in North Vietnam.

The Military Revolutionary Council (as the Military Revolutionary Committee had been renamed after the coup of Jan. 30) met on Aug. 14-16 at the seaside resort of Cap Saint-Jacques; Major-General Duong Van Minh, the nominal Chief of State, did not attend, stating that he was ill. The Council unanimously approved on Aug. 16 a new Constitution, described as the "National Charter", which established a presidential system of government on the American model. Its main provisions were as summarized below.

(1) The preamble stated that "fundamental individual liberties and democratic institutions cannot be exercised and established in their integrity immediately, but will progressively come into effect as the situation develops. The armed forces' mission to guide the nation will end as soon as the situation permits, and will then be transferred to the people's elected representatives."

(2) The Military Revolutionary Council, representing the armed forces, would be the supreme political body. It would elect the President and the Vice-President, the president, vice-president, and members of the Provisional National Assembly, and the president of the High Council of Judges.

(3) Executive powers were vested in the President. If national independence and

the integrity of the national territory were urgently threatened, he would "make all decisions and take all appropriate measures, after consultation with the president of the Provisional National Assembly and with the approval of the Military Revolutionary Council".

(4) Legislative powers were vested in the Provisional National Assembly, which would consist of 50 representatives of the armed forces and 100 civilians. The President would have the right of veto, and could be overridden by a three-quarters majority of the Assembly.

(5) Judges would be appointed by the President, the independence of the judiciary being guaranteed.

(6) The new national institutions would be established within a month of the promulgation of the Constitution.

After the adoption of the Constitution General Nguyen Khanh was elected President by 50 votes out of 58 cast. Lieut.-General Tran Thien Khiem (the Defence Minister and C.-in-C.) received five votes, and Major-Generals Duong Van Minh and Do Cau Tri (commander of the 2nd Army Corps) one each, whilst there was one blank vote.

At a press conference later the same day General Nguyen Khanh said that although elections could not yet be held, one-third of the Assembly would be chosen from the members of the municipal and provincial councils, which would be elected later, and another third from members of political and other organizations. Political parties which assisted in the fight against Communism would be allowed to continue, but all those which did not co-operate with the Government would be eliminated. He stated that General Duong Van Minh would continue to act as an adviser to the Revolutionary Council.

The political changes were adopted after consultations with General Maxwell Taylor (the U.S. Ambassador, who had taken up his post on July 2) and other senior American officials, who were believed to have given their approval.

Buddhist and Student Demonstrations against the Regime

The new Constitution, with its provisions for continued military rule and dictatorial powers for General Nguyen Khanh, aroused widespread opposition, especially among the Buddhist community and the students. The Buddhists resented the removal from power of General Duong Van Minh, the leader of the coup which overthrew the Government, and the fact that officers who had suppressed Buddhist demonstrations against the former regime, such as General Do Cau Tri, retained their commands; they

55

also alleged that persecution of Buddhists by some Government officials still continued. Feeling was intensified by the anniversary of the raids on Buddhist pagodas on Aug. 21, 1963 [see page 42], with the result that demonstrations to commemorate this anniversary developed into demonstrations against the Government.

On Aug. 21 several hundred students demonstrated in Saigon, denouncing the Government as "a military dictatorship worse than Diem's dictatorship," and presented a petition demanding elections within three months, the restoration of government by civilians, abrogation of the "National Charter," relaxation of the state of emergency, freedom of the Press, academic freedom, and a purge of former officials of President Diem's regime. General Nguyen Khanh received a student delegation on the following day, and the same evening Saigon Radio announced that their grievances had been satisfied; on Aug. 23, however, students sacked the radio station, demanding that this report should be officially denied. Catholic refugees from North Vietnam, who had been brought into Saigon for the purpose and were led by Government officials, burnt down the headquarters of the Vietnamese Students' Association on Aug. 24; a few hours later students stormed the Ministry of Information and forced the Deputy Minister to promise that the censorship would be relaxed.

Even more violent disturbances, which frequently assumed an anti-Catholic and sometimes an anti-American character, were meanwhile taking place in several provincial towns.

Neither in Saigon nor elsewhere did the police or troops make any attempt to suppress public meetings or demonstrations, although these were illegal under the emergency regulations, or even to suppress acts of violence. In part this was attributed to the Government's fear that the use of force against the demonstrators might provoke a popular uprising, but it was also believed that the Government was uncertain how far it could rely upon the troops; at Danang paratroopers looked on while students murdered Catholics and set fire to houses, and even mingled with the rioters.

Annulment of New Constitution – Resignation of President Nguyen Khanh

In the late evening of Aug. 24 Thich Tam Chau and two other Buddhist leaders presented to General Nguyen Khanh an ultimatum demanding *inter alia* a new Constitution, civilian rule, free elections by November 1965, and the punishment of former officials of the Diem regime. The general promised to meet their demands and during the night he had a conversation lasting several hours with General Taylor. A Government communiqué issued on the morning of Aug. 25 announced that General Nguyen Khanh was holding conversations with a view to the formation of a new Government, and that the Aug. 16 Constitution would be revised, the duration of the curfew reduced, the censorship relaxed, and mistakes by local authorities punished. The terms of the communiqué were strongly resented by the Buddhists, who asserted that General Nguyen Khanh had broken his promise to grant all their demands.

Shortly afterwards about 20,000 people, the majority students and schoolchildren, took part in a procession through Saigon, nominally in memory of a girl student shot by President Diem's police a year before. The demonstrators finally assembled outside the Presidential Palace, demanding General Nguyen Khanh's resignation, the abolition of the new Constitution, the ending of military rule, a purge of corrupt officials and freedom of the Press. The general himself addressed the crowd, assuring them that he was on their side if their proposals were "patriotic, anti-Communist and anti-dictatorial," and shouted "Down with dictatorship, including Communist dictatorship!" At the crowd's request he also shouted "Down with dictatorship, including military dictatorship," but withdrew angrily when they repeated their demand for the abolition of the new Constitution. At 1.15 p.m. it was announced through loudspeakers that the Constitution had been annulled, but the demonstrators refused to disperse until their other demands had also been granted. Shortly afterwards it was announced that General Nguyen Khanh had resigned the Presidency, and that the Revolutionary Council would dissolve itself after electing a new Chief of State, who would summon a National Convention.

The communiqué was received with jubilation by the demonstrators, who thereupon dispersed peacefully. At Hué, however, student demonstrators the same evening demanded the dissolution within 24 hours of the Revolutionary Council, which, they declared, had no right to choose the new Chief of State, and the punishment of General Nguyen Khanh and other military leaders as allegedly former members of the *Can Lao* [the semi-secret political organization formerly led by Ngo Dinh Nhu, of which General Nguyen Khanh denied that he had ever been a member] .

The Revolutionary Council failed to reach agreement on a new Chief of State on Aug. 26, and resumed its discussions on the following day. During the morning about 3,000 Catholics armed with knives, hatchets, iron bars and bottles assembled outside the Army headquarters, where the meeting was taking place, demanding that the Council should retain power, cheering General Nguyen Khanh and denouncing General Duong Van Minh. When they tried to storm the building the troops opened fire, some firing into the air and others into the crowd, six of whom were killed.

Faced with the imminent threat of anarchy, the Council agreed to dissolve itself and to transfer power to a Provisional Leadership Committee composed of Generals Nguyen Khanh, Duong Van Minh, and Tran Thien Khiem, with General Nguyen Khanh as Prime Minister of a caretaker Government. The Council's final communiqué stated: "The Republic of Vietnam armed forces will return to their purely military mission of protecting the nation and fighting Communism, neutralism, colonialism and all forms of dictatorship and betrayal. The present Government will temporarily carry on the affairs of the nation and will convene a National Convention within two months. The National Convention is entrusted with the task of electing a provisional leader for the nation and establishing ... national institutions which will oppose Communism, neutralism, and colonialism."

The formation of the Provisional Leadership Committee was believed to be a compromise intended to conciliate both Buddhist and Catholic opinion and to ensure U.S. support. As General Tran was supported by the Catholics and General Duong by the Buddhists, it had been proposed that the former should become Chief of State with the latter as Prime Minister; U.S. officials, however, were reported to have warned the Council that continued American support was dependent upon General Nguyen Khanh's remaining in authority.

Riots in Saigon

Street fighting between Buddhists and Catholics broke out in Saigon during Aug. 27. Appeals were issued by the Provisional Leadership Committee and jointly by the Buddhist Secular Institute and the Archbishopric of Saigon to both communities to remain calm and

58

maintain order. The riots nevertheless continued on Aug. 28, becoming increasingly savage. Numerous arrests were made by the troops and police, who once opened fire to disperse a crowd, though without causing any casualties; as a result of these measures order was restored by Aug. 29.

General Nguyen Khanh Resumes Premiership

The political situation meanwhile remained extremely confused. A press conference which the members of the Provisional Leadership Committee were to have addressed on Aug. 28 was cancelled for unexplained reasons, and instead General Nguyen Khanh made a press statement to the effect that he had submitted his resignation as President and Prime Minister on the previous day, but had received no reply; that he enjoyed the support of the Buddhist leaders, the Archbishop of Saigon and the armed forces; and that he was prepared to play any part with which the people chose to entrust him.

On Aug. 29 it was announced that Dr. Nguyen Xuan Oanh (the Second Vice-Premier) had been appointed acting Premier for a maximum period of two months, with the task of convening a National Congress representing all political parties, religious communities, and sections of the country, which would elect a provisional Chief of State. Dr. Nguyen Xuan Oanh, an economist by profession and a Buddhist by religion, was not associated with any political faction; he lived in the United States for many years, returning to South Vietnam only after the overthrow of the Diem regime.

Dr. Oanh told a press conference on Aug. 29 that General Nguyen Khanh, who had left for Dalat, needed a long period of rest and medical treatment; there was no question of deterioration in the general's mental condition, he added, but he was "more sick mentally than physically". General Taylor, however, stated on Aug. 31 that General Nguyen Khanh would return to Saigon within a few days to resume his duties. Dr. Nguyen Ton Hoan resigned from the Government on Sept. 1, stating that he found it impossible to continue working with General Nguyen Khanh, and left the country on Sept. 6.

The unrest among the Buddhists and students meanwhile continued. A communiqué issued by Buddhist leaders in Saigon on Aug. 31 gave warning that if the Government had not granted the people their liberties by Oct. 27 [the end of the two

59

months' period referred to in the Revolutionary Council's communiqué of Aug. 27 —
see above], a general strike would begin on that date and Buddhists would adopt a
policy of non-co-operation. Under pressure from the Buddhist leaders, who had
threatened to begin a hunger strike if their demands were not granted, the
Government released on Sept. 2 all the 509 persons arrested during the riots; police
officials alleged that these included 11 known Viet Cong leaders.

Student leaders in Saigon announced on Aug. 31 that demonstrations would be
suspended for two months, but would be resumed if the membership of the proposed
National Congress proved unacceptable. At Hué, where the student strike continued,
Buddhist professors of the university set up on the same day a "People's
Revolutionary Committee", which announced that it would organize a National
Convention to elect a civilian Government, whilst at Danang the students'
association issued a statement denouncing General Nguyen Khanh's replacement by
Dr. Nguyen Xuan Oanh as "a bluff leading to the re-establishment of the
dictatorship".

General Nguyen Khanh returned to Saigon on Sept. 3 to resume the
Premiership, and began a series of talks with Buddhist, Catholic and
student leaders. General Duong Van Minh, however, flew on the same
day to Hué, where he announced his support for the programme of the
People's Revolutionary Committee; the committee reaffirmed its opposition to General Nguyen Khanh's "illegal" Government, but declared
itself satisfied with General Duong's explanations on his own position.

At a press conference on Sept. 4 General Nguyen Khanh claimed
that, although his health was not yet restored, he had resumed the
Premiership "at the request of the principal generals and the religious
and political groups." All the other military members of the Government, he announced, had resigned — viz., General Tran Thiem Khiem,
General Do Mau (Third Vice-Premier) and General Lam Van Phat.

General Nguyen Khanh also gave details of a plan for the restoration of
democratic government, for which, he claimed, he was solely responsible, and
which the other members of the Provisional Leadership Committee had not yet
approved. During the first phase, which would end not later than Oct. 27, General
Duong would convene a council of representatives of leading religious and political
groups, which would designate a committee of lawyers to draft a temporary
Constitution and would also convene a National Congress. In the second phase the
Congress would nominate a National Assembly, which would act as a legislative
body and draft a permanent Constitution; this would be submitted to a national
referendum for approval, possibly by the end of 1965. He himself, General Nguyen
Khanh stated, would automatically resign at the end of the first phase.

Government Changes

It was announced on Sept. 8 that the Provisional Leadership Committee had chosen General Duong Van Minh as its chairman, and that he

would exercise the powers of Chief of State but would not resume the title. He would also convene a High National Council, which would appoint a new Government and draft a new Constitution.

At a press conference on Sept. 9, at which all three members of the Provisional Leadership Committee were present, General Nguyen Khanh announced that he himself would take over the Defence portfolio in addition to the Premiership; that Dr. Nguyen Luu Vien (a prominent opponent of President Diem's regime) had been appointed Minister of the Interior; and that Tran Van Huong had been appointed Prefect of Saigon *vice* Brigadier-General Duong Ngoc Lam (a supporter of the Dai-Viet). He also announced that the Press censorship had been abolished, and that Major-Generals Tran Van Don, Le Van Kim, Ton That Dinh, Mai Huu Xuan and Nguyen Van Vy had been placed at the disposal of the Defence Ministry—a measure equivalent to their reinstatement in the Army. The five generals, who had been arrested after the Jan. 30 coup on charges of "neutralism", had been released on May 30 but held under surveillance at Dalat.

Abortive Military Coup in Saigon

A group of right-wing and Catholic officers, several of whom had associations with Dai Viet, attempted to carry out a military coup in Saigon on Sept. 13. In the early hours of the morning about 2,000 troops from the Mekong delta sector, led by Major-General Duong Van Duc, commander of the 4th Army Corps, moved into the capital and occupied the Prime Minister's office, police headquarters, the radio station, the central post office, and other key positions without meeting any resistance. General Nguyen Khanh was in Dalat at the time; of the other members of the Provisional Leadership Committee, General Tran Thien Khiem flew there to join him, whilst General Duong Van Minh remained in Saigon.

The coup was believed to have been precipitated by the proposed reinstatement of the five generals of the "Dalat group" [see above], for whose arrest in January General Duong Van Duc had been responsible, and by the imminent transfer from the delta sector of two largely Catholic regiments, on whose support the conspirators relied. Many of the officers involved had recently been removed from their commands or from Government posts, including Generals Lam Van Phat and Duong Ngoc Lam, Colonels Nhan Minh Trang and Huynh Van Ton and Lieut.-Colonel Duong Hieu Nghia.

As the mutineers advanced on and occupied Saigon, Air Force planes flew overhead without attacking; the mutineers therefore believed they were supplying air support to them, but Air Commodore Nguyen Cao Ky, commander of the Air Force, stated afterwards that his pilots had wished to attack the advancing troops but that he had forbidden them to do so in order to prevent bloodshed.

Shortly after noon General Lam Van Phat, as spokesman for the mutineers, made a broadcast calling for the arrest of General Nguyen Khanh, whom he accused of treason and corruption and of failing to conduct the war against the Viet Cong successfully, and announced the formation of a "People's Council for the Salvation of the Nation". His violent attack on the Prime Minister was believed to have been made on his own initiative and to have been contrary to the wishes of the other rebel leaders, who hoped to open negotiations with General Nguyen Khanh. The Prime Minister replied in a broadcast from Dalat, calling on the armed forces to support him against the mutineers.

Following General Phat's broadcast, Commodore Nguyen Cao Ky adopted an openly hostile attitude towards the mutineers. Although General Duong Van Duc attempted to win his support through negotiations conducted by radio, he gave warning that his aircraft would go into action if the mutineers moved against the Saigon air base, while fighter-bombers flew low over points held by the mutineers in an obvious threat to bomb them.

At about 4 p.m. General Duong Van Duc made a broadcast on behalf of the "People's Council for the Salvation of the Nation" which was much more moderate in tone than General Phat's. Without attacking General Nguyen Khanh, he stated that the objects of the coup were to re-establish national unity and the Government's prestige, to carry out a purge of "traitors" and to end interference in State affairs by political parties and religious bodies. General Nguyen Van Thieu, who apparently had taken no part in the coup, was sent to Dalat to negotiate with General Nguyen Khanh; Dalat Radio afterwards broadcast a message of support for the Prime Minister by General Tran Thien Khiem, who stated that he also spoke for General Nguyen Van Thieu.

About 10 p.m. General Nguyen Khanh flew back to Saigon and began talks at the air base with Commodore Nguyen Cao Ky and

62

General Cao Van Vien, the Chief of Staff. They were joined by Mr. Alexis Johnson (the U.S. Deputy Ambassador) and General Joseph Moore (the American commander of the 2nd Air Division), and later by General Duong Van Minh; General Taylor had been on his way back from Washington when the coup took place, and did not arrive in Saigon until the early hours of Sept. 14.

Saigon Radio announced at midnight that General Nguyen Khanh again had the situation in hand. After his talks with the Prime Minister, Commodore Nguyen Cao Ky began negotiations at the air base with General Duong Van Duc and other leaders of the coup; General Lam Van Phat was not present. As a result an agreement was reached whereby the mutineers withdrew from Saigon in the early hours of Sept. 14.

Commodore Nguyen Cao Ky, General Duong Van Duc and other Army, Navy and Air Force officers appeared together at a press conference at 10 a.m.; among those present was Sub-Brigadier-General Nguyen Chanh Thi (leader of the unsuccessful coup of November 1960), who had played a key role in the defeat of the previous day's coup by rallying the 1st and 2nd Army Corps to the support of the Government. General Duong Van Duc stated that the 4th Corps had taken action because of "the return of neutralist elements [presumably the 'Dalat group' of generals] to the capital and the presence of pro-Communist elements in the Administration". Air Commodore Nguyen declared that there had not been a coup; what had happened had been "the result of the aroused patriotism of members of the armed forces," who now "understood".

A resolution which the officers present had sent to the Government was read to the press conference. It demanded that within the next two months the Government should dismiss all corrupt officers and civil servants and severely punish profiteers, otherwise "the people and the armed forces will again be compelled to make a second revolution."

General Duong Van Duc, who had been kept under surveillance in Saigon, was arrested on Sept. 15 and relieved of his command, which was transferred to General Nguyen Van Thieu. General Duong Ngoc Lam, Colonel Huynh Van Ton and Lieut.-Colonel Duong Hieu Nghia were arrested on the following day, whilst General Lam Van Phat, who had left Saigon with the mutineers, gave himself up to the police.

General Tran Thien Khiem Leaves Vietnam

The Government announced on Sept. 30 that General Tran Thien Khiem would leave the following day on a mission to a number of

63

countries which were providing aid to South Vietnam, and that General Nguyen Khanh would assume the functions of C.-in-C. in his absence.

According to unofficial reports, the General's removal had been demanded by the Buddhist leaders and by a group of young generals who had supported the Government against the attempted coup. After delaying his departure for several days, he finally left on Oct. 7 and was appointed Ambassador to the United States on Oct. 29.

Acquittal of Leaders of Attempted Coup

The trial of the leaders of the Sept. 13 coup on charges of attempting to overthrow the Government opened before a military court on Oct. 15. The accused, all of whom pleaded "not guilty," included three generals, 10 colonels and lieutenant-colonels, and seven civilians, among them Tran Quoc Buu, the Roman Catholic president of the Vietnamese Confederation of Labour.

All the accused were acquitted on Oct. 23, but General Nguyen Khanh ordered the officers concerned to be detained for periods of up to 60 days for offences against military discipline, and announced that they would be "allowed" to leave the Army.

General Tran Van Don was appointed Deputy C.-in-C. on Nov. 14, with General Ton That Dinh as his assistant; General Nguyen Van Vy became chief of General Nguyen Khanh's personal staff; and General Mai Huu Xuan head of the Army's newly created psychological warfare department. These appointments, and the light sentences on the leaders of the coup, were interpreted as an attempt by General Nguyen Khanh to reconcile the opposing factions in the armed forces.

Provisional Constitution Adopted by High National Council

The High National Council, consisting of 17 prominent public figures nominated by General Duong Van Minh, met in Saigon on Sept. 26 to draft a provisional Constitution, and elected Phan Khac Suu as its chairman. The other members included representatives of the Buddhist, Roman Catholic, Caodaist and Hoa Hao communities, and also Dr. Le Khac Quyen and Professor Ton That Hanh, president and vice-president of the People's Revolutionary Committee at Hué [see page 60]. The

64

Council promulgated on Oct. 20 a provisional Constitution, the main features of which were as follows:

Sovereignty. Sovereignty would be exercised by the people's elected representatives. Owing to the present situation, however, a National Convention would be convened in accordance with procedure to be defined by law.

Fundamental Rights. Equality before the law and freedom of thought, speech, the Press, religion, assembly, and association were guaranteed, but freedom of speech might not be "abused ... to make propaganda for Communism or neutralism".

Freedom to establish trade unions and the right to strike were recognized, but civil servants and employees of essential public services were forbidden to strike.

Chief of State. The Chief of State, to be selected according to procedure to be defined by the National Convention, would appoint the Prime Minister, after obtaining the National Convention's approval; would preside at Cabinet meetings; and would appoint the C.-in-C. after consultation with the Prime Minister.

If the independence and integrity of the national territory were threatened, the National Convention might empower the Chief of State to legislate by decree for a limited period.

Legislature. The legislative power was vested in the National Convention.

The National Convention might censure Ministers or the Government as a whole by a vote of two-thirds of its total membership; if it censured the Prime Minister it must nominate his successor. If it passed a vote of no confidence in two Cabinets within 12 months, the Chief of State might dissolve it; he must then convene within 40 days a new National Convention, which might not be dissolved for a year.

Judiciary. To guarantee the independence of judges, their transfer and disciplinary penalties would be decided by a High Council of the Magistracy.

Special Councils. An Economy and Welfare Council would be established, which must be consulted by the Government and the National Convention on all Bills affecting the economy or social welfare.

A National Security Council, consisting of the Chief of State, Prime Minister, Minister of the Armed Forces, and C.-in-C., would propose declarations of war, cessations of hostilities, and proclamations of a state of emergency or martial law, and would review and approve defence policy.

High National Council. Until the establishment of the National Convention, the High National Council would exercise the Convention's powers, and after its establishment would act as a second Chamber.

Cabinet Formed by Tran Van Huong

The High National Council unanimously elected Phan Khac Suu as Chief of State on Oct. 24. He accepted on condition that he should hold the post only until the National Convention met, and was officially installed on Oct. 26.

On the same day, President Suu accepted the resignation of the Provisional Leadership Committee and the Government of General Nguyen Khanh, who was subsequently appointed C.-in-C. on Nov. 4. The President called upon Tran Van Huong, the Prefect of Saigon, on Oct. 30 to form a Government, the composition of which aroused widespread criticism. Dr. Nguyen Xuan Chu, who had succeeded Phan Khac Suu as chairman of the High National Council, resigned on Nov. 5 on the grounds that the Council should have been consulted on the choice of Ministers and that it contained too many officials who had been "closely associated with previous unpopular regimes, notably that of Ngo Dinh Diem." Le Van Thu, a lawyer, was elected chairman of the High National Council on Nov. 18.

The Buddhist and student leaders announced their opposition to the Government on Nov. 6, whilst the Press was almost unanimously hostile. Tran Van Huong, however, declared on Nov. 5 that any anti-Government demonstrations would be suppressed, and that General Nguyen Khanh had assured him of the Army's support; the General himself commented on the following day that the Army would not try to resume power "unless the situation demands it". About 5,000 demonstrators who marched to the Presidential Palace on Nov. 22 demanding the dismissal of the Government were dispersed by the police, who used tear-gas and made a bayonet charge.

VI. THE CHALLENGE OF THE NATIONAL LIBERATION FRONT (N.L.F.) – FOREIGN REACTION

From 1960 onwards, Communist-led guerrilla warfare in South Vietnam increased; as a result, military and economic aid from non-Communist countries was sought by the South Vietnamese Government. American involvement in Vietnam increased during 1960-64 and many other countries responded, to varying degrees, to the South Vietnamese appeal for aid.

The National Liberation Front, 1960-64

At a secret conference held in Cochin China in December 1960 the various guerrilla organizations in South Vietnam agreed to unite in the National Liberation Front, the main points in its programme being as follows:

(1) Replacement of Ngo Dinh Diem's regime by "a Government of national and democratic union composed of representatives of all social classes, all nationalities, the various political parties and all religions"; election of a new National Assembly; freedom of the press, assembly, trade unionism, religion and party organization; a general amnesty for political prisoners.

(2) Development and modernization of industry and agriculture; suppression of monopolies; limitation or prohibition of imports that the national economy was capable of producing; reduction of import duties on raw materials and machinery; improvement of the workers' living and working conditions.

(3) Reduction of land rent; the fixing of an upward limit for land holdings; the purchase at fair prices of lands exceeding this limit for free distribution among peasants with no or insufficient land.

(4) The progressive reunification of Vietnam by peaceful means on the basis of negotiations between the two zones. Pending reunification, the repudiation by the two Governments of propaganda and military activities against each other, and the encouragement of economic and cultural exchanges and freedom of travel, trade, and correspondence between the two zones.

The leading element in the Front was the Revolutionary Party of Labour (the South Vietnamese Communist Party), founded in 1962, but its supporters also included many members of the Hoa Hao and Cao Dai sects, which had continued armed resistance to President Diem's regime in the Tayninh area after the suppression of these sects in 1955-56. The president of the Front, Nguyen Huu Tho, was a non-Communist Saigon lawyer who was imprisoned by Diem's Government from 1954 to 1961, when he escaped; the general secretary, Nguyen Van Hieu, was a Communist journalist and a former professor of history. The central committee of the Front also included representatives of the Buddhists, the Catholics and the tribal peoples.

The Paris newspaper *Le Monde* published in August 1963 an account of the organization and policy of the N.L.F. given by a member of its central committee. The N.L.F. leader stated:

"We have not yet formed any national organization for the administration of the liberated zones. At present there are only popular associations electing local provisional committees. We are thinking of setting up a national provisional committee soon, but it will not be established until after the Front has been broadened politically, by agreement with other members of the Opposition. Contacts have been established even with representatives of the Army and with private individuals, living in this country or abroad. The conduct of military operations is directed by the central committee, under which are regional committees corresponding to the different zones. . . ."

On the Front's policy he said: "There is no question of installing a people's democracy in the South, at least not as you understand the term. There will be no nationalization for the present. We shall be able to consider coolly the case of important foreign enterprises, especially French enterprises, which play such a large part in the South Vietnamese economy. We are ready to begin talks on equal terms with the representatives of foreign interests. . . . In the political field we ask only for the end of the dictatorship, free and fair elections in which all the country's political organizations and social categories will take part, the progressive withdrawal of the U.S. troops, and co-operation on equal terms with all countries wishing to help us. Our foreign policy will be based on neutrality and refusal to join military blocs."

After admitting that for a long time the Front had hoped for military aid from

North Vietnam, he said: "In the long run we prefer to settle our affairs between ourselves—that is, between Southerners. Certainly aid from the North would be useful, but it is not our first preoccupation and will not be the decisive element in our struggle. Besides, the distance and the lack of logistic infrastructure mean that it will never be important. We have not struggled for years, in the worst conditions, to replace one dictatorship by another. We cannot accept dependence on the North. Certainly we hope that the country will be reunited one day. But that will be possible only in the distant future, for to start with the two regimes will be very different. . . . We think that the point of view put forward by people outside the Front like Tran Van Huu, which would postpone the problem of reunification for 15 or 20 years, is realistic and acceptable."

Hanoi Radio broadcast on Oct. 5, 1963, a letter recently sent to the United Nations by the leaders of the Front proposing the following conditions for a peaceful settlement: (1) withdrawal of all U.S. military aid to President Diem's Government; (2) negotiations between South Vietnamese of all political tendencies without foreign participation; (3) free elections and the formation of a coalition Government.

In his first interview with a foreign journalist, published in *Le Monde* on July 21, 1964, Nguyen Huu Tho said: "We are ready . . . to enter into discussions with all parties, groups, sects and patriotic individuals, regardless of political differences or past activities, in order to reach a peaceful solution of the problem of South Vietnam on the basis of national independence, democracy and neutrality. . . . South Vietnam's internal affairs must be settled by the Vietnamese themselves, which excludes all foreign interference. The basis of any eventual agreement must be the withdrawal of all American troops, arms and war materials from South Vietnam. The Front is not opposed to an international conference to facilitate the search for a solution, but the role of the foreign Powers participating in a conference must be confined to suggestions, registration of the agreement between all the interested Vietnamese parties, and guarantees for its implementation. . . . We are ready to conclude an alliance, backed with material and military aid, with any group which agrees with the essential points of our programme . . . even if there are differences on other points. . . .

"Reunion with the North," Nguyen continued, "must be achieved step by step, by means of negotiations between the responsible authorities of the North and the South. . . . The re-establishment of cultural, economic, commercial and postal relations between the two zones and the exchange of family visits must constitute the first necessary steps towards the normalization of relations. . . ."

Operations against the guerrilla forces of the "National Liberation Front", which was referred to in Government statements as the Viet Cong (Vietnamese Communists), continued throughout the period 1962-64.

According to foreign estimates, the strength of the Viet Cong forces remained constant during this period at between 20,000 and 30,000

69

regulars; as their casualties were heavy (they were estimated at 30,000 killed in 1962 and 20,500 in 1963), this meant that they were more than replacing their losses. Mr. McNamara stated on March 26, 1964, that the "hard core" were supported by 60,000 to 80,000 irregulars, but estimates given by British Correspondents put the number of auxiliaries and Viet Cong agents among the population as high as 200,000 to 300,000. It was believed that the commanders of the regular battalions were mostly Vietminh veterans of Southern origin who had gone to North Vietnam after 1954 and had since returned, but that the rank and file were entirely from South Vietnam.

In addition to Chinese weapons, including mortars and heavy machine-guns as well as large quantities of ammunition, the Viet Cong were armed with American or French equipment captured from Vietnamese Army stores or from strategic hamlets which they had raided, but they also used home-made weapons such as shotguns made from gas piping. The Chinese weapons were believed to have been imported by junks via the Mekong delta, which was largely controlled by the guerrillas, or over the land route from North Vietnam through the Vietminh-controlled areas in Laos (the "Ho Chi Minh trail").

Increased United States Aid to South Vietnam, 1964

General Maxwell Taylor (then chairman of the U.S. Joint Chiefs of Staff) arrived in Saigon on May 11, 1964, for talks with the Vietnamese Government, and was joined by Mr. McNamara on the following day.

After receiving their report on these discussions, President Johnson sent a message to Congress on May 18 requesting an additional $55,000,000 for military and $70,000,000 for economic aid to South Vietnam.

The President said that since the 1964-65 Budget was prepared in January, two major changes had occurred in South Vietnam: the Viet Cong had intensified their activities, and General Nguyen Khanh had put forward proposals to expand the armed forces and the civil administration. These and other measures would require an increase of about 40 per cent in South Vietnam's domestic Budget expenditures; the country's revenues could not be increased proportionately, and severe inflation resulting from a Budget deficit would endanger political as well as economic stability, unless offsetting financial actions were taken.

70

In view of the deterioration in the political and military situation, General Maxwell Taylor again flew to Washington on Nov. 26 to discuss with the U.S. Administration the events in South Vietnam and the future prosecution of the war against the Viet Cong. After extensive talks with President Johnson, Mr. Rusk, Mr. McNamara, and other high U.S. officials, the following statement was issued from the White House on Dec. 1:

"The President reviewed the situation in South Vietnam with Ambassador Taylor and with the Secretaries of State and Defence, the Director of Central Intelligence, and the Chairman of the Joint Chiefs of Staff.

"Ambassador Taylor reported that the political situation in Saigon was still difficult, but that the new Government under Prime Minister Huong was making a determined effort to strengthen national unity, to maintain law and order, and to press forward with the security programme, involving a combination of political, economic, and military actions to defeat the Viet Cong insurgency. The Ambassador also reported that, although the security problems have increased over the past few months in the Northern provinces of South Vietnam, with uneven progress elsewhere, the strength of the armed forces of the Government was being increased by improved recruiting and conscription, and by the nearly 100 per cent increase in the combat strength of the Vietnamese Air Force. Also, the Government forces continue to inflict heavy losses on the Viet Cong.

"On the economic front Ambassador Taylor noted that agricultural output was continuing to increase, with U.S. assistance in fertilizers and pesticides playing an important role. He also noted that the prices of goods and the value of the piastre have remained remarkably stable. On the other hand, the Ambassador reported that increased interdiction of the communication routes by the Viet Cong is interfering to some extent with commerce within the country, and recent typhoons and floods in Central Vietnam have destroyed a large percentage of the crops and livestock in that region. The Vietnamese Government, with U.S. assistance, has moved promptly to organize a programme which is bringing relief and rehabilitation to the stricken areas.

"The meeting reviewed the accumulating evidence of continuing and increased North Vietnamese support of the Viet Cong and of North Vietnamese forces in, and passing through, the territory of Laos in violation of the Geneva Accords of 1962. The President instructed Ambassador Taylor to consult urgently with the South Vietnamese Government as to measures that should be taken to improve the situation in all its aspects.

"The President reaffirmed the basic U.S. policy of providing all possible and useful assistance to the South Vietnamese people and Government in their struggle to defeat the externally supported insurgency and aggression being conducted against them. It was noted that this policy accords with the terms of the Congressional Joint Resolution of Aug. 10, 1964, which remains in full force and effect." [The Resolution of Aug. 10 reaffirmed U.S. willingness to help in defending freedom in South-East Asia and its readiness to reply to any attack upon American forces; it also confirmed and reinforced the powers of the Presidency in any action the President considered necessary.]

71

Other Foreign Military and Economic Aid to South Vietnam, 1964

It was announced in Washington on May 13 that the U.S.A. and South Vietnam had appealed to 25 free-world countries to start or to increase military or economic aid to the Republic of Vietnam. In a further appeal to 34 Governments on July 14 General Nguyen Khanh again asked for increased aid to South Vietnam, in view of "the considerable expansion of the means and forces brought into play by the aggressors".

Military aid in the form of personnel and equipment was received from Australia and South Korea. These two countries together with Italy, Japan and the Philippines also gave medical aid to South Vietnam. Economic aid was given by several countries—Formosa, France, West Germany, Japan, New Zealand, Persia, Siam and the United Kingdom—and Canada, France and West Germany gave aid in the educational field.

In addition, the South Vietnamese Foreign Ministry stated on Oct. 3 that economic or technical aid had already been granted or promised by India and the Netherlands, and that Belgium, the Irish Republic, Malaysia, Spain, Switzerland, and Tunisia were studying the possibility of social and economic aid to South Vietnam.

VII. PROLONGED POLITICAL INSTABILITY – NOVEMBER 1964 - SEPTEMBER 1965

The political situation in South Vietnam remained highly unstable throughout this period owing to the repeated intervention in politics of the armed forces, organized in a newly-formed Armed Forces Council. This body dissolved the High National Council (the nominated legislature) on Dec. 20, 1964, and overthrew Tran Van Huong's civilian Government on Jan. 27, 1965, after Buddhist leaders had organized a campaign of mass demonstrations against it. A new Cabinet was formed on Feb. 16 by Dr. Phan Huy Quat. An attempted coup by a group of officers in Saigon on Feb. 19 collapsed for lack of support; immediately afterwards, however, the Armed Forces Council removed General Nguyen Khanh from his post as C.-in-C., replacing him by General Tran Van Minh, and forced him to leave the country. The civilian Government led by Dr. Phan Huy Quat decided on June 11 to hand over power to the military leaders, following a prolonged constitutional crisis which was intensified by Catholic agitation against the Government. A military junta headed by Major-General Nguyen Van Thieu then took power, and on June 19 a Cabinet was formed by Air Vice-Marshal Nguyen Cao Ky, commander of the Air Force.

Heavy fighting between the Government and Viet Cong forces meanwhile continued, notably in the Saigon sector and in the central highlands.

Buddhist and Student Demonstrations against Government

Thousands of Buddhists, most of them students, demonstrated against Tran Van Huong's Government on Nov. 22, 1964, being forcibly dispersed by the police who used tear-gas and arrested many of the demonstrators. As a result the Buddhist leaders, who had not sponsored the demonstrations and had hitherto reserved their attitude towards the Government, adopted an openly hostile attitude towards it. Thich Tam Chau (president of the Buddhist Institute for Secular Affairs) submitted an ultimatum to President Phan Khac Suu and the High National Council on Nov. 24, demanding the Government's resignation and the release of the arrested demonstrators.

New demonstrations in Saigon on Nov. 25 developed into serious riots in which students stoned the police, while the police and troops used tear-gas and fired on the crowd with pistols. A 15-year-old boy was killed in the rioting, and according to official figures 85 soldiers and policemen and 25 civilians were injured.

Martial law was imposed on Saigon on the same day; the curfew was extended from three to seven hours, all schools and university faculties closed, public meetings and strikes banned, and the press, radio and newsreels placed under censorship. A state of siege was proclaimed on Nov. 26, Brigadier-General Pham Van Dong being appointed military governor of the city. The press censorship was strictly enforced, 10 newspapers being suspended on Nov. 26 and four more on the following day.

The High National Council, in a communiqué issued on Nov. 27, called on the Prime Minister to consider reshuffling his Cabinet, and to endeavour to avoid bloodshed while maintaining order. Thich Tam Chau, however, declared on Nov. 28 that the Buddhists would continue to oppose the Government even if it were reshuffled, and demanded the release of all those arrested during the riots; he also stated that "the Buddhists will not oppose the will of the people if they demand the ending of the war." The funeral on Nov. 29 of the boy killed in the riots was the occasion for new demonstrations which were dispersed by troops, about 100 people being arrested. The curfew was shortened to five hours on Dec. 3, and primary schools allowed to reopen on the following day.

Buddhist Allegations of Persecution

In a statement on Dec. 10 the Buddhist leaders alleged that the Government was employing secret agents of President Ngo Dinh Diem's regime, suppressing Buddhist newspapers and supporting the anti-Buddhist Press, and requiring officials to state their religion, with the aim of purging Buddhists from the Civil Service. A law promulgated on Dec. 14 authorized the formation of the General Association of Vietnamese Buddhism, a pro-Government organization opposed to the Buddhist Institute.

It was announced on Dec. 16 that the Minister of Education, Phan Tan Chuc, who had been strongly criticized by the Buddhists, had resigned and had been succeeded by Nguyen Van Truong, a leading educationist who had been imprisoned by President Diem's regime in 1963 because of his Buddhist opposition activities.

Formation of Armed Forces Council –
Dissolution of High National Council

From December onwards an increasingly prominent role in politics was played by a group of younger generals, which had been largely responsible for the defeat of the attempted coup on Sept. 13, 1964 [see page 61], and was popularly nicknamed the "Young Turks" [a reference to the officers' organization which dominated Turkish politics during the years 1908-1914]. Its leaders were Brigadier-General Nguyen Chanh Thi, commander of the 1st Army Corps and leader of the military revolt of November 1960, and Air Vice-Marshal Nguyen Cao Ky, commander of the Air Force.

It was reported on Dec. 6 that the group had presented General Nguyen Khanh with an ultimatum, demanding that he should give his support to the Government or resign by Dec. 15.

On behalf of the group, General Khanh requested President Phan Khac Suu on Dec. 17 to retire about 40 senior officers, including General Duong Van Minh and the generals of the "Dalat group" [see page 61]. The President referred the request to the High National Council, which refused to accept it. On the following day 30 generals formed an Armed Forces

75

Council, with General Nguyen Khanh as chairman, to advise the latter in his capacity as C.-in-C. on major decisions affecting the armed forces.

The Armed Forces Council on Dec. 20 declared the High National Council dissolved and arrested six of its members, including Le Van Thu, the chairman, and Tran Van Van, the general secretary. A proclamation issued by the Armed Forces Council, while expressing its confidence in and support for President Phan Khac Suu and Tran Van Huong's Government, accused the High National Council of "being abused by counter-revolutionary elements" and of "hampering the reorganization of the armed forces".

The U.S. Ambassador, General Maxwell Taylor, had a private meeting on Dec. 21 with General Nguyen Khanh at which he was reported to have warned him that the United States considered the present position untenable. General Nguyen Khanh, however, issued an Order of the Day on Dec. 22 expressing his full approval of the coup, and in which he declared that "although the armed forces support a clean civilian Government, when necessary they still have the task of acting as an intermediary to settle all disputes and differences. . . ." The Order added: "We make sacrifices for the country's independence and the Vietnamese people's liberty, but not to carry out the policy of any foreign country. . . . Better to live poor but proud as free citizens of an independent country rather than in ease and shame as slaves of the foreigners. . . ". In another statement General Nguyen Khanh asserted that General Taylor's activities had been "beyond imagination so far as an ambassador is concerned," and that if the U.S. Ambassador "does not act more intelligently the United States will lose South-East Asia".

The U.S. State Department issued the following statement on Dec. 22: "Ambassador Taylor has been acting throughout with the full support of the U.S. Government. As we have repeatedly made clear, a duly constituted Government exercising full power on the basis of national unity and without improper interference from any group is the essential condition for the successful prosecution of the effort to defeat the Viet Cong, and is the basis of U.S. support for that effort. This is the position Ambassador Taylor has been expressing to Vietnamese leaders."

President Phan Khac Suu and M. Tran Van Huong, who had previously made no public statement since the coup, issued a communiqué on Dec. 28 which said: "The event of Dec. 20 shook the solution of civilian government. . . . Because of the lack of a legislative body constituting the legal basis for the present regime, the executive agencies no longer fully represent the government by civilians. . . . For the past week we have made and are still making strenuous efforts to find a way to conciliate divergent views, to preserve the solidarity binding the Government, the armed forces and the people, while saving full civilian government. . . . We hope that, thanks to the warm support of the entire population and to the goodwill of the generals on the Armed Forces Council, we will find a fitting solution."

Agreement between Government and Armed Forces Council

After prolonged negotiations between the Armed Forces Council, the Government, and the U.S. Embassy, a compromise agreement was reached on Jan. 9, 1965, its terms being as follows:

(1) The armed forces reaffirmed the pledges contained in their proclamation of Aug. 27, 1964 [see page 58].

(2) The Government would speedily convene a National Convention, representing all sections of the population, which would assume the legislative power.

(3) The Chief of State was temporarily invested with the legislative power until the Convention met.

(4) The persons "temporarily isolated by the armed forces" would be released.

Government Changes

Two Ministers criticized by the Buddhists resigned and four officers entered the Cabinet on Jan. 18, General Nguyen Van Thieu becoming Second Deputy Premier and Air Vice-Marshal Nugyen Cao Ky, Minister for Youth and Sports.

Renewed Anti-Government and Anti-American Demonstrations by Buddhists

However, at the beginning of January 1965 the Buddhist leaders had renewed their agitation against the Government, which had been suspended since the coup of Dec. 20. Buddhists and students demonstrated in Saigon on Jan. 4 in protest against the proposed trial by court-martial of the students arrested on Nov. 29, a number of people being injured in clashes with the police. Hué was brought to a standstill on Jan. 7 by a general strike organized by the Buddhists, the Viet Cong taking advantage of the situation to raid the suburbs of the town.

After the agreement of Jan. 9 [see above] the Buddhist campaign assumed an increasingly anti-American character; leaflets circulated in Saigon accused the Americans of having "imposed" the agreement to keep their "servile collaborator Tran Van Huong" in power, and declared that "the Vietnamese people claims the right to democratic self-determination". Hué was again paralysed on Jan. 11-12 by a general strike, which was also widely supported in Danang and Quangtri, and a series of anti-Government demonstrations took place at Dalat during Jan. 16-19.

In Saigon parachute troops and police clashed with demonstrators outside the Buddhist Institute on Jan. 20, and made 24 arrests. Two days later troops and police used tear-gas and clubs to break up a demonstration outside the U.S. Embassy; a section of the crowd then stoned the U.S. Information Service library, and running battles with the police continued into the night. In the riots 223 people were arrested and many injured, including about 60 Buddhist monks and nuns. The U.S. Information Service library at Hué was sacked on Jan. 23 by a mob which stormed the building and destroyed 8,000 books. A communiqué issued by the Buddhist Institute on the same day denounced Tran Van Huong as a "lackey" of General Taylor, alleged that the latter was seeking to exterminate the Buddhists, and called upon Buddhists to follow the example of Thich Quang Duc, the first monk to burn himself to death in the campaign against President Ngo Dinh Diem [see page 40].

On Jan. 25 about 20,000 people took part in a protest march at Hué during which students attacked the homes of the chief of police and the head of the Vietnamese Information Service, and 71 people were arrested in Saigon after a clash between demonstrators and the police, who used tear-gas. Later the same day Hué was placed under martial law, and the death penalty ordered for terrorists in Saigon. On Jan. 26 a 17-year-old girl burned herself to death at Nha Trang, in the first fire suicide for political reasons since October 1963; students attempted to seize the radio station at Hué; 40 monks who tried to demonstrate at Gia Dinh (outside Saigon) were dispersed by the police with tear-gas; and other attempted demonstrations in the capital were broken up.

Government Overthrown by Armed Forces Council

The Armed Forces Council carried out a new coup in Saigon on Jan. 27, when it removed Tran Van Huong from office. A resolution adopted

78

by the Council claimed that the civilian Government was "not able to cope with the supremely important needs of the present emergency situation"; withdrew the Council's support from the President and the Government; and entrusted General Nguyen Khanh with "the task of solving all the present political crises".

At a press conference on Jan. 28 General Khanh announced, however, that President Phan Khac Suu had agreed to remain Chief of State and would retain his legislative power. He also announced that the Armed Forces Council had appointed Dr. Nguyen Xuan Oanh (the Third Deputy Premier) as acting Prime Minister; and that the rest of the Cabinet would retain their posts until a new Government was formed. Tran Van Huong resigned later the same day and subsequently took refuge in the British Embassy, fearing that his life was in danger from the Buddhists.

The State Department said on Jan. 28 that endorsement of the new regime would be withheld until the structure of the new Government was clarified, but that the United States would support a Government which commanded the support of the people. President Johnson's special assistant for international security affairs, Mr. McGeorge Bundy, paid a visit to South Vietnam from Feb. 4-7 during which he had talks with military, political and religious leaders. After returning to Washington, he expressed the opinion that the contending political and religious factions were "working out" an understanding and that there were "strong forces working towards the establishment of an effective Government".

Formation of New Cabinet

A new Cabinet was formed on Feb. 16 by Dr. Phan Huy Quat; this was intended to be as representative as possible and included members of 12 of South Vietnam's 18 political groups. It contained four Catholics, among them General Nguyen Van Thieu and Lu Van Vi, a Caodaist, Dr. Le Van Hoach, and a representative of the Hoa Hao sect; all the other Ministers were Buddhists, but only Ngo Trong Anh and Tran Quang Thuan had been associated with the Buddhist political movement. Eight of the Ministers were of North Vietnamese origin.

National Legislative Council

In a statement on Feb. 16 the Armed Forces Council said that, as the situation required a sound administration immediately, it had taken upon itself the responsibility of appointing the Chief of State and Prime Minister and would set up a transitional legislative body. "The procedures and time to convene the National Congress," the statement added, "as well as the duties of this body, will be later considered and defined by the Legislative and Executive"—an intimation that the elections, fixed for March 21, might be postponed. The statement added that "after the Legislative and Executive are set up the Armed Forces Council will return to its military position", and that the Armed Forces Council would "act as an intermediary whenever necessary in order to preserve equilibrium until there is a Government elected directly by the people. . . ".

The Armed Forces Council appointed on Feb. 17 a National Legislative Council of 20 members to act as a transitional legislature, with Major-General Pham Xuan Chieu as its chairman. This body consisted of six officers, four professors, two lawyers, two doctors, and six other civilians, and included representatives of the main regions of Vietnam and the four leading religious communities.

Attempted Military Coup in Saigon

Troops led by Colonel Pham Ngoc Thao, previously South Vietnamese press attaché in Washington, temporarily seized control of Saigon on Feb. 19. The political aims of the attempted coup, apart from the removal from power of General Khanh, were uncertain but the Colonel was reported to favour negotiations with the Viet Cong in an attempt to isolate the Communist elements in its leadership. He was supported by a group of right-wing and Roman Catholic officers, many of them former supporters of President Ngo Dinh Diem who had been dismissed from the Army for taking part in the attempted coup of Sept. 13, 1964; these included Brigadier-General Lam Van Phat, Colonels Huynh Van Ton and Nhan Minh Trang, and Lieut.-Colonel Duong Hieu Nghia.

Troops of an armoured battalion, supported by infantry and marines, seized control of the General Staff and naval headquarters, the radio station, the telephone exchange, the airport, and other key points in the early afternoon of Feb. 19, and by 3.30 appeared to be in effective control of Saigon. Orders for the arrest of General Khanh, Air Vice-Marshal Ky, and Admiral Cang could not be carried out, however, since General Khanh had escaped to Vung-Tau (Cap St. Jacques) by air shortly before the rebels seized the airport; Air Vice-Marshal Ky was at Bien Hoa air base, and Admiral Cang ordered the fleet to leave Saigon to prevent the rebels from capturing it.

In a broadcast at 2.15, Colonel Pham Ngoc Thao denounced General Khanh as a "dictator" and claimed that the coup had the support of Lieut.-General Tran Thien Khiem (the South Vietnamese Ambassador in Washington), who, he stated, would return to Saigon. General Khiem, however, in a press statement in Washington, denied all previous knowledge of the coup though expressing approval of the rebels' aims; he said that he would return to Saigon if he was needed, but that the situation was "fluid" and there was much confusion.

Negotiations were conducted by telephone between General Lam Van Phat and Air Vice-Marshal Ky, who threatened to bomb the airport and General Staff headquarters if the rebels did not evacuate them. To emphasize this threat, fighter-bombers flew over the city; after General Westmoreland (commander of the U.S. forces in South Vietnam) had appealed to Air Vice-Marshal Ky not to bomb the airport, where 6,500 U.S. troops were stationed, the latter agreed to postpone any such action until 7 a.m. on the following day. General Westmoreland also arranged a meeting at Bien Hoa between Air Vice-Marshal Ky, General Lam Van Phat, and Colonel Pham Ngoc Thao, at which the rebel leaders repeated their demand for the removal of General Khanh from his command.

General Khanh meanwhile made a tour of Army posts in the Mekong delta, rallying support against the rebels, and in a broadcast denounced General Lam Van Phat and Colonel Pham Ngoc Thao as former members of President Diem's *Can Lao* organization [a semi-secret élite corps within the National Revolutionary Movement which combined political and police functions]. In the evening troops converged on Saigon from both north and south, and by midnight had reached the suburbs. At 6.30 a.m. on Feb. 20 parachute troops from Bien Hoa and Vung-Tau occupied the radio station without meeting any opposition, and during the morning the airport, the telephone exchange, and the Staff headquarters were also reoccupied. By noon the rebel troops, who had put up virtually no resistance, had withdrawn from the city and their leaders had gone into hiding. The Armed Forces Council issued an order for the arrest of General Lam Van Phat, Colonel Pham Ngoc Thao, and 13 other officers, but gave an assurance that the rank and file would not be punished.

The General and the Colonel were sentenced to death by a military court on March 7, and Colonels Huynh Van Ton and Truong Van Chuong to life imprisonment; all four were tried *in absentia*. Thirty-three officers and civilians, most of them Catholics, were arrested on May 21, 1965, on charges of conspiring to overthrow the Government; the plot was reported to have been formed by the group responsible for the Feb. 19 coup, under the leadership of Colonel Pham Ngoc Thao. Colonel Huynh Tan Hung, who had been sentenced to 20 years' imprisonment *in absentia* for complicity in the coup, was shot dead while resisting arrest.

General Tran Van Minh Appointed C.-in-C. –
General Khanh leaves Vietnam

A meeting of 15 members of the Armed Forces Council held at Bien Hoa during the morning of Feb. 20 reaffirmed its support for the Government, but adopted a resolution of no confidence in General Khanh by majority vote. General Nguyen Chanh Thi, who had been reported on Feb. 5 to be demanding General Khanh's removal, and who had flown to Bien Hoa from Hué on learning of the coup, was believed to be primarily responsible for this development. After the meeting General Khanh flew to his command post at Vung Tau.

The situation remained tense throughout Feb. 21, as it was feared that General Khanh would attempt to regain power by force; the Council mustered forces near Saigon, and General Nguyen Chanh Thi gave warning that any troop movements by supporters of General Khanh would be bombed. In the evening the Council unanimously voted to remove him from his command and to appoint General Tran Van Minh, acting C.-in-C.; this decision was officially confirmed by President Phan Khac Suu shortly afterwards. On learning of the vote General Khanh telephoned a number of divisional commanders, offering them promotion in return for their support, but without success.

In the early morning of Feb. 22 General Khanh flew to Dalat, from where he informed the Council by telephone of his decision to accept the loss of his command, and on the following day President Phan Khac Suu signed a decree appointing General Khanh a roving Ambassador. The latter returned to Saigon on Feb. 24, and after formally handing over his command to General Tran Van Minh left for Hong Kong on Feb. 25; it was stated that his first task would be to present evidence to the U.N. that the Viet Cong revolt was being directed from North Vietnam. His virtual exile completed the elimination from public life of the triumvirate who had dominated South Vietnamese politics during the year following President Diem's overthrow—Generals Duong Van Minh, who was living in Bangkok, Tran Thien Khiem, and Nguyen Khanh—and left the "Young Turks" [see page 75] in control of the situation.

The Armed Forces Council on March 3 elected five of its members to act as its governing committee, which would replace General Khanh in the leadership of the Council. The committee consisted of General Nguyen Van Thieu, who was appointed its general secretary, Air Vice-Marshal Nguyen Cao Ky, General Cao Van Vien, General Pham Van Dong and General Van Cao.

Widespread Agitation for Peace

A strong movement in favour of a cease-fire, peace negotiations and the reunification of Vietnam developed during February and March, with both Buddhist and Caodaist support. At a press conference in Saigon on Feb. 25 the leaders of a newly-formed Peace Movement issued the text of a resolution which had been signed by 358 leading intellectuals and public figures, calling for immediate cease-fire negotiations between the Government and the National Liberation Front, the withdrawal of all U.S. troops from South Vietnam, and respect for the Geneva Agreements. Thirty-eight of the signatories were arrested, among them Dr. Nguyen Xuan Bai, the father of Dr. Nguyen Xuan Oanh; three of them—Dr. Pham Van Huyen (a former commissioner for the resettlement of refugees from North Vietnam), Cao Minh Thien and Professor Ton That Duong—were deported to North Vietnam on March 19.

On Feb. 28 a second organization, the Struggle Movement for Peace and Unity, was inaugurated at a conference in Cholon, and a steering committee appointed with Thich Quang Lien (director of the cultural affairs office of the Buddhist Institute) as chairman to organize a campaign in favour of peace.

The manifesto of the movement, which it was proposed to send to the South and North Vietnamese Governments, called on both to "cease immediately their dirty war". Emphasizing that the Vietnamese question must be settled by the Vietnamese themselves, it declared that "the Vietnamese people do not want their country to become one of the Sino-Russian satellites or a colony of the Western imperialists", and put forward the following demands: (1) the disbanding of the National Liberation Front and the withdrawal of all leading Communists to North Vietnam; (2) the withdrawal of all U.S. troops from the South and of all Soviet and Chinese advisers from the North; (3) the formation of a reconciliation committee to help the South and North Vietnamese Governments to bring about the peaceful reunification of the country.

At a press conference on March 1 Dr. Phan Huy Quat declared that the war in South Vietnam was "obviously a war of self-defence" and that the

Government would not accept "a mere truce which the Communists could exploit"; it would therefore take "all necessary measures to smash the fallacious propaganda manoeuvres that the Communists are waging with a view to deceiving public opinion." The Prime Minister, who stated that leaders of the Buddhist Institute had denied to him that they were connected with the Struggle Movement for Peace and Unity, subsequently informed Thich Quang Lien on March 4 that he had no objection to his movement's sending its proposals or even a delegation to Hanoi, but that the Government would not associate itself with any such approach.

A peace plan resembling Thich Quang Lien's in many respects was published on March 16 by the influential Cao Dai sect. This proposed a cease-fire; the provisional withdrawal of the Communist element in the N.L.F. to North Vietnam pending general elections; the formation of a reconciliation committee; and the federation of North and South Vietnam. The U.S. troops should be regrouped along the frontiers, and withdrawn when peace had been restored; if fighting broke out again, the U.N. should be asked to send an international police force to Vietnam. A press conference in Saigon, called by the Caodaist leaders to launch their peace campaign, was broken up on March 17 by the police and the sponsor of the plan arrested.

Dismissal of Admiral Chung Tan Cang

A mutiny took place in the fleet at Saigon on April 8, when Rear-Admiral Chung Tan Cang (commander of the Navy) was arrested by four of his officers, who accused him of malfeasance. There was no serious violence, but as a precaution Air Vice-Marshal Nguyen Cao Ky ordered fighters to fly low over the city. It was announced on the following day that Admiral Cang and Brigadier-General Pham Van Dong (commander of the Saigon military district) had been suspended pending an investigation of corruption charges against them.

The suspension of Admiral Cang, a Catholic, aroused unfavourable reactions in Catholic circles, which feared that it was the prelude to a general purge of Catholic military commanders, and on April 12 a delegation from the hierarchy appealed to the Prime Minister, Dr. Phan Huy Quat, to intervene. Dissatisfaction with the Government was already

84

widespread among the Catholic community in the Saigon area, where priests had organized an armed Catholic militia. At an interview on April 8 General Maxwell Taylor was reported to have urged Mgr. Nguyen Van Binh, the Archbishop of Saigon, to calm his co-religionists.

Dissolution of Armed Forces Council

The Armed Forces Council announced on May 6 its decision to dissolve itself, in view of "the progress achieved by the civilian Government" and because it was "time for all officers to devote themselves entirely to the conduct of the war against the Viet Cong". General Nguyen Van Thieu tendered his resignation as Deputy Premier and Armed Forces Minister on the same day, but it was not accepted.

Resignation of Government – Military Junta Takes Power

Dr. Phan Huy Quat announced a number of Cabinet changes on May 25, whereby Tran Van Thoan became Minister of the Interior, Nguyen Trung Trinh Minister of the Economy, Dinh Trinh Chinh Minister of Information, Lam Van Tri Minister of Agriculture, and Tran Thanh Hiep Minister of Labour. This announcement gave rise to a constitutional crisis, as two of the Ministers whom it was proposed to replace—Nguyen Hoa Hiep (Interior) and Professor Nguyen Van Vinh (Economy)—refused to resign. President Phan Khac Suu thereupon refused to confirm the proposed changes unless the two Ministers resigned or the National Legislative Council passed a vote of no confidence in them, whilst the Council informed Dr. Quat on May 26 that it saw no reason to pass such a vote.

The political crisis led to a revival of the Catholic agitation against the Government. A Catholic delegation presented a petition to the President on May 27 demanding the dismissal of Dr. Phan Huy Quat, whom they accused of religious discrimination and seeking to co-operate with neutralists and French "colonialists". Clashes between Catholics and the police occurred on June 5, and on the following day anti-Government demonstrations took place in Saigon.

After the political deadlock had continued for a fortnight without any solution being reached, Dr. Quat announced on June 9 that he had asked the generals to act as mediators between himself and his opponents. At a joint meeting of the President, the Cabinet, the National Legislative

85

Council and the military leaders on June 11, it was unanimously decided that the President, the Cabinet and the Council should all resign and hand over power to the generals. The military leaders were reported on June 13 to have decided to form a three-man junta, with Air Vice-Marshal Nguyen Cao Ky as chairman; this plan was believed to have been dropped on June 14, however, as a result of representations by General Maxwell Taylor, who had just returned from consultations in Washington. A ruling committee of 10 generals, calling itself the "Committee for the Direction of the State", was formed later the same day under the chairmanship of General Nguyen Van Thieu who became in effect Chief of Staff. In a proclamation he denied that the Army intended to impose a dictatorship, and undertook to "hand over power to the people's elected representatives the day security and order are re-established, liberty assured, and the Communists completely crushed".

Air Vice-Marshal Nguyen Cao Ky was nominated by the junta to form a Government, but his appointment met with objections both from Buddhist and Catholic leaders, who favoured the appointment of a civilian Premier, and from the U.S. authorities, nominally on the ground that he could not combine the Premiership with the command of the Air Force; their real objections, however, were believed to be to his impulsive temperament and lack of administrative experience. He stated on June 17 that he intended to give up his Air Force command.

New Cabinet – Declaration of State of War Proposed

The new Cabinet (the ninth to hold office since November 1963) was formed on June 19, with Air Vice-Marshal Nguyen Cao Ky as Prime Minister.

A new Constitutional Charter published on June 19, which replaced the provisional Constitution of Oct. 20, 1964, provided that the Cabinet would be responsible to the Committee for the Direction of the State, which would lay down the policies to be applied; the Committee, however, would itself be responsible to a Congress of the Armed Forces, composed of all the general officers and commanders of the various specialized branches. A National Security Council, consisting of the chairman and secretary of the Military Directorate, the Prime Minister, the War Minister

86

and the Chief of Staff, was empowered to propose the proclamation of a state of emergency.

In a statement on taking office, Air Vice-Marshal Ky said: "The war against the Communist forces supported by North Vietnam is going badly. Political confusion is accompanied by a growing feeling of insecurity; the economy is collapsing; injustice reigns; and war profiteers are flourishing." He therefore proposed to declare a state of war, introduce an austerity regime, and mobilize the whole country's potential. All men capable of bearing arms would be conscripted, and armed units would be formed to maintain security in the rear. Special courts would be set up, and would inflict heavy penalties on profiteers and other delinquents.

Addressing representatives of the leading religious and political groups on June 17, Air Vice-Marshal Ky said that he would not tolerate resistance to his policies, and that if his opponents failed to end their hostile activities he would shoot their leaders.

Disturbances broke out at Hué after the Government issued a mobilization decree on Aug. 12 making all men under 37 who held the *baccalauréat* (the qualification for admission to a university) liable to military service. Student demonstrations began on Aug. 21, and spread to the nearby towns of Quangtri and Danang. Although the Government modified the decree, demonstrations continued daily, the students being joined by many adult members of the Buddhist community. About 4,000 people took part in an anti-government rally on Aug. 29, at which the speakers, who included members of the city council and the provincial council, denounced General Nguyen Van Thieu as a "Fascist," accused him of attempting to set up a military dictatorship and misappropriating public funds, and demanded that the military regime should be replaced by an elected civilian Government.

Decrees issued on Sept. 3 authorized the Government to create military zones in which it would have the power to search private houses by day or night, ban strikes and public meetings, censor the Press, and close all places of public entertainment. This would enable the Government to extend to any part of the country the martial law regulations already in force in Saigon, Hué, Danang and other towns.

Cabinet Changes

The Prime Minister, Air Vice-Marshal Nguyen Cao Ky, carried out a Cabinet reshuffle on Oct. 1, 1965. The most important change was that Brigadier-General Nguyen Huu Co (the War Minister) also became

Vice-Premier with responsibility for the co-ordination of the pacification programme, several Ministries, including those of Public Works and Rural Affairs, being placed under his control.

More sweeping changes were made on Feb. 21, 1966; a number of new departments—those of Revolutionary Development, Ex-Servicemen, Refugees, Montagnard Affairs, Supply, and Ports—were created to deal with economic and social problems arising from the war with the Viet Cong, and the Ministry of Communications was separated from that of Public Works.

Paul Nur, the first Montagnard to be appointed to a high Government post, entered the Cabinet on Feb. 21, 1966, as Special Commissioner for Montagnard Affairs. In a broadcast on Feb. 26 he stated that his department had been created to accelerate projects for the betterment of the Montagnards' living conditions, and appealed to them to help realize a new Vietnamese society in which different racial groups would merge into a single national entity.

The Montagnards, who number between 500,000 and 1,000,000, are divided into at least 20 tribes, all distinct from and hostile to the Vietnamese. Large-scale Vietnamese settlement in the Central Highlands began only after 1954, and was bitterly resented by the Montagnards. While some of the Montagnards co-operated with the Viet Cong, others had been successfully organized by U.S. advisers into Special Forces for service against the guerillas. In recent years the "Unified Front for the Struggle of the Oppressed Races" (FULRO), which demanded autonomy for the 12 northern provinces, had won strong support among the Rhade (one of the more advanced tribes, who live in the region around Ban-Me-Thuot), and an unsuccessful revolt took place in September 1964.

At the beginning of August 1965, FULRO supporters surprised a Special Forces camp near Ban-Me-Thuot, carried off a store of arms, and were joined by about 200 of the Special Forces; after troops had been sent to the area on Sept. 10, however, 411 of the rebels surrendered without attempting to resist. A more serious revolt broke out on Dec. 17, when tribal troops seized control of Phu Thien (a district capital in Phu Bon province), were 34 people were killed, and Gia Nghia (capital of Quang Duc province); attempted uprisings also occurred in three other provinces, apparently as part of a co-ordinated plan. All the revolts were suppressed, in some cases after heavy fighting, and four of the leaders publicly shot at Pleiku on Dec. 29; fighting nevertheless continued in Phu Bon, where many of the rebels had succeeded in escaping into the jungle.

VIII. CONTINUED BUDDHIST RESISTANCE
TO MILITARY GOVERNMENT

Dismissal of General Nguyen Chanh Thi — Protest Demonstrations

By a unanimous decision of the other nine members of the Committee for the Direction of the State (the ruling military junta, generally referred to as the Directory), General Nguyen Chanh Thi was removed on March 10 from his command, which embraced the five northern provinces of South Vietnam, on the ground that he was acting independently of the Government, especially in administrative matters. This decision was reported to have been approved beforehand by the U.S. Ambassador, Mr. Henry Cabot Lodge.

General Thi's dismissal was followed by protest demonstrations in the northern cities of Danang and Hué, in which troops and police played a prominent part. As the movement spread to Saigon and other cities it was increasingly directed against the military junta and in favour of free elections and civilian rule, and assumed a strongly anti-American character.

The most important political force involved in the agitation was the United Buddhist Church, and especially its Institute for the Propagation of the *Dharma* (Vien Hoa Dao), which deals with secular affairs. Although the 86-year-old Thich Tinh Khiet is the nominal head of the Church, its main political leaders were four younger monks—Thich Tam Chau, director of the Vien Hoa Dao, regarded as a moderate; Thich Tri Quang, the leader of the more militant faction; and his close associates Thich Thien Minh, commissioner for youth affairs of the Vien Hoa Dao, and Thich Ho Giac, the Church's most powerful orator.

Another factor contributing to the crisis was the strong regionalist feeling in Central Vietnam (formerly Annam), and particularly in Danang (formerly Tourane), the second largest city in South Vietnam, and Hué, the former capital of Annam. Both cities were centres of resistance to the Saigon Government during the Buddhist campaign against President Ngo Dinh Diem in 1963 and the agitations against military rule in August 1964 and August 1965 [see pages 39, 55, 87].

The widespread anti-American feeling which became apparent during the crisis was attributed to both political and economic factors. The educated classes considered that the United States was gradually eroding South Vietnamese sovereignty, and the strong support given to Marshal Ky by President Johnson at the Honolulu Conference had caused him to be regarded as an American "stooge". The Americans were also considered responsible for the inflation, which had made it difficult for civil servants, junior officers and soldiers to support their families. [The Honolulu Conference was held from Feb. 4 to Feb. 8, 1966, between the South Vietnamese leaders and U.S. military and diplomatic representatives in Vietnam. In a joint communiqué issued at the conclusion of discussions, it was stated that "the leaders of the two Governments reached full agreement upon a policy of growing military effectiveness and of still closer co-operation between the military forces of Vietnam and those of the United States".]

Demonstrations against General Thi's dismissal began in Danang on March 11 and in Hué on the following day, and on March 15 Danang was paralysed by a general strike. General Thi, who had at first been forbidden to return to his former headquarters at Danang, was allowed to do so on March 16, in the hope that he would discourage further agitation. After receiving an enthusiastic welcome in both Danang and Hué, however, he announced on March 18 that he was prepared to "join the Army and the people in the fight for a civilian Government and social justice".

A manifesto issued by the Vien Hoa Dao on March 12 demanded that all generals who had done "meritorious service for the revolution" should be restored to their positions; that all generals serving abroad or at home should return to their purely military duties; and that a National Assembly

90

and "a Government that brings about national unity" should be established. Thich Tri Quang asserted in an interview on March 15 that Marshal Ky's "rotten" Government had remained in power only because of "the support of other people", and that Marshal Ky himself had become "more hated" since the Honolulu Conference.

Buddhist demonstrations started in Saigon on March 16, when Thich Ho Giac, addressing about 10,000 people, declared that the demand for civilian rule would be realized "whatever the cost". Thich Tam Chau, on the other hand, denied in a conciliatory speech on March 19 that the Buddhists had any essential differences with the junta or wished to overthrow the Government. Marshal Ky, however, greatly offended the Buddhists when he declared on the same day that the Government would not be influenced by demonstrations and strikes, and would not yield to "unjustified claims which are contrary to the people's interests". The Vien Hoa Dao sharply criticized this statement on March 21 as "hasty and unconstructive".

In Danang and Hué a general strike began on March 23, accompanied by mass demonstrations at which the speakers and the banners carried by the demonstrators accused the United States of "interfering" in Vietnamese affairs and opposing the introduction of constitutional government. The rebels received the full co-operation of the local authorities; the mayor of Danang, Dr. Nguyen Van Man, granted the students written permission to take over the radio station, and the police prevented strike-breakers from going to work.

Concessions Made by the Directory

The growing unrest forced the junta to make a number of concessions. Marshal Ky announced on March 25 that a committee would be appointed within a week to draft a Constitution within two months, and that after the Constitution had been approved by a referendum general elections would be held as soon as possible. On the following day he stated that the committee would consist of members of the elected provincial councils and of representatives of religious, political and professional groups, and that elections might take place before the end of 1966. The Directory approved these proposals on March 30; it did not make clear, however, whether the committee would be elected, as the Buddhists demanded, or nominated. It also decided to "take all appropriate disciplinary measures against officials and soldiers who continue to take part in activities harmful to public order and national security".

These concessions failed to end the anti-Government agitation, which spread on March 25 to Nhatrang. About 20,000 people, including at least 1,000 junior officers and soldiers in uniform, took part in an anti-American demonstration in Hué on March 27, and about 10,000 Buddhists staged a similar demonstration in Saigon on March 31. Thich Tam Chau, however, dissociated himself from this demonstration, which, he said, had been organized by Thich Thien. Minh. Roman Catholic leaders meanwhile put forward demands on March 29 for the formation of a civilian Government, whilst at the same time calling for the suppression of the Buddhist agitation in Central Vietnam.

Government's Threat to Use Force against Opposition — Widespread Anti-Government Demonstrations

At the beginning of April the agitation in Central Vietnam developed into open revolt. When Lieut.-General Pham Xuan Chieu (general secretary of the Directory) arrived in Hué on April 1 in an attempt to persuade General Thi to return to Saigon he was detained by student leaders and held virtually as a prisoner, being released on the following day only as a result of General Thi's intercession. Thousands of troops and police took part in mass demonstrations in Danang and Hué on April 2, and General Thi openly announced his opposition to the Directory for the first time.

Anti-Government agitation was intensified in Saigon during April 2-4, and spread to other leading towns not previously affected.

Marshal Ky announced on April 3 that troops would be sent to "liberate" Danang, which he alleged was under Communist control, and threatened to shoot Dr. Nguyen Van Man, whom he accused of using public funds to pay demonstrators as well as others connected with an anti-Government "struggle committee". Lieut.-General Nguyen Van Thieu (chairman of the Directory) alleged in a broadcast on the following day that Communists had infiltrated the anti-Government demonstrations in an attempt to seize power; he gave warning that the state of war promulgated in June 1965 remained in force, and ordered all schools to be closed. He also announced that a "National Political Council" would be convened in the immediate future, with a view to "finding solutions based on extended consultations with the people".

Two battalions of Marines were flown from Saigon to Danang during the night of April 4-5, some of them in aircraft supplied by the U.S. forces, but did not leave the air base. Inside the town troops of the 1st Army Corps erected road blocks and placed machine-guns on all the roads to the base, and the population armed themselves with sticks and stones in readiness to resist the pro-Government troops. Marshal Ky himself flew to Danang air base on April 5, but fighting was averted by General Nguyen Van Chuan, the commander of the 1st Army Corps who had an interview with Marshal Ky at the base and warned him that any attempt by the Marines to enter Danang city could lead to bloodshed. Marshal Ky thereupon made a broadcast apologizing to the people of Danang, and stating that General Chuan had convinced him that he was mistaken in believing that the city was Communist-controlled.

Anti-Government demonstrations meanwhile continued. In Hué the local commander, Major-General Phan Xuan Nhuan, announced his opposition to the Government and promised to arm the students; in view of the grave situation in the town it was decided to evacuate all U.S. civilians. In Saigon about 20 people were injured when thousands of Buddhist demonstrators clashed with the police. Rioting also occurred at Nhatrang, where the U.S. Information Service library was burnt down, and at Pleiku.

Deadlock Reached between Government and Buddhists – Further Demonstrations

On returning to Saigon later on April 5 Marshal Ky met the Buddhist leaders and promised that elections to a Constituent Assembly would be held shortly. The Buddhist leaders accordingly agreed to suspend demonstrations, and on April 6 temporarily closed the Vien Hoa Dao headquarters; Buddhist demonstrators nevertheless attacked the offices of a pro-Government newspaper later the same day, several being wounded when troops charged them with fixed bayonets.

A National Political Council convened by the Government met in Saigon on April 6, but was boycotted by the Buddhist and Catholic leaders invited. In a letter to the Buddhist leaders Marshal Ky promised on the same day that an elected Constituent Assembly would meet within four to six months. The Vien Hoa Dao issued a communiqué on April 7 demanding as a condition for a tentative truce with the Government that this promise should be officially confirmed by a decree of the Directory;

that no action should be taken against soldiers and officials who had opposed the Government; that all arrested demonstrators should be released; and that the troops sent to Danang should be evacuated by April 11. The communiqué also called on Buddhists to suspend demonstrations pending the Government's reply, and announced that a delegation would be sent to Danang and Hué to explain the Church's position.

The Directory did not meet the Buddhist terms, some of which were described as misrepresenting what Marshal Ky had offered; moreover, it was believed that its members were themselves divided over the policy to be pursued, especially the withdrawal of the Marines from Danang. General Nguyen Huu Co had announced on April 6 that the evacuation of the Marines would begin on the following day, but a request for the use of U.S. aircraft for this purpose was subsequently reversed without explanation. Government aircraft flew low over Danang on April 7-8 as a show of force, despite protests by General Chuan. In consequence the situation in the northern cities remained tense; in Danang a group of officers claiming to represent the entire staff of the 1st Army Corps issued a declaration of no confidence in the Government, and in Hué the students, who were being given military training by the Army, rejected the Buddhist leaders' proposal for a political truce, demanding Marshal Ky's immediate resignation. All U.S. civilians were evacuated from Danang on April 9.

General Chuan, whose attitude had aroused the Directory's suspicions, was recalled to Saigon on April 8. Lieut.-General Ton That Dinh, who had played a prominent part in both President Ngo Dinh Diem's persecution of the Buddhists and the coup which led to the President's overthrow, was appointed commander of the 1st Army Corps on April 9, and took up his post on the following day.

In Saigon the situation greatly deteriorated on April 8 after pro-Government soldiers had thrown hand-grenades into the pagoda used as the Vien Hoa Dao headquarters. Thousands of youths, led by Buddhist monks, demonstrated in favour of peace with the Viet Cong and a civilian Government, and the mobs attacked U.S. servicemen and civilians, 10 of whom were injured. Fighting between security forces using batons and tear-gas and students throwing stones and Molotov cocktails continued throughout the night.

94

In view of the junta's reluctance to compromise, the Buddhist leaders formed a "Struggle Movement Committee" on April 9, with Thich Thien Minh and Thich Ho Giac as its joint chairmen, to co-ordinate their followers' activities. In a statement issued on the following day the committee accused Marshal Ky of having "brutally betrayed" them in their campaign for a civilian Government, and declared that "a civil war that will take tens of thousands of lives and cause the total collapse of national unity may well take place because of the short-sightedness, irascibility, and irresponsibility of the present Government". At a press conference Thich Thien Minh refused to rule out the possibility that the Buddhists, if they came to power, would negotiate with the National Liberation Front and demand the withdrawal of the U.S. forces.

National Political Congress – Government's Promise to Hold Elections to a Constituent Assembly

The Directory announced on April 8 that a National Political Congress, composed of 48 chairmen of provincial and municipal councils and about 120 representatives of religious, political and professional organizations, would meet on April 12 to "sound out the aspirations of the people of all social strata in view of the setting up of a Constituent Assembly". On April 10 the Government began withdrawing its Marines from the Danang base.

When the National Political Congress met in Saigon on April 12 it was boycotted by the Buddhist and Catholic organizations; only 92 of those invited were present, and 20 of these walked out almost immediately, but an additional 23 joined the congress on April 13. Addressing the congress on April 12, General Thieu declared that the Directory shared the people's desire for an elected Government in the shortest possible time. In Danang and Hué soldiers and police took part in demonstrations against the congress, which was denounced as unrepresentative and as "a tool of the U.S. Central Intelligence Agency".

At its final session on April 14 the congress adopted the following political programme, which in effect met the Buddhists' demands:

(1) The military Government should promise to resign as soon as a Constituent Assembly was elected.

(2) The Government should promulgate a decree providing for elections within four months, and the Constituent Assembly should be empowered to turn itself into a legislative body.

(3) The Government should convene a commission within ten days to draft an electoral law.

(4) The Government should take measures to prevent Communists and neutralists from infiltrating the Constituent Assembly.

(5) Freedom of the Press should be granted.

(6) The Government should create favourable conditions for the development of political parties.

(7) The Government should launch a campaign to educate the masses in democracy.

(8) The Government should grant an amnesty to all those involved in the agitation against it, and should use political, not military, solutions in rebellious areas such as Danang and Hué.

(9) All religions and parties should end demonstrations.

(10) All factions should work for national unity.

The Directory announced its acceptance of this programme on the same day, and promulgated a decree-law providing for elections to a Constituent Assembly within three to five months "through universal, direct, and secret balloting throughout the territory of the Republic of South Vietnam". Dr. Than Quang Dan, chairman of the National Political Congress, said in a press statement on April 15 that in accordance with the decree-law of April 6 a council would be set up to draft an electoral code and supervise the elections.

The Buddhist leaders announced on April 15 that they would suspend their agitation, but would renew the struggle if the Government tried to punish agitators and if the organization of the elections was not fair. In a speech in Hué on April 18 Thich Tri Quang appealed for the ending of demonstrations, and gave a warning that if they continued the Government might resign in order to "create anarchy" and thereby prevent the holding of elections. A general meeting of students subsequently voted in favour of accepting this advice, while reserving the right to resume demonstrations if the Government did not keep its undertakings.

Government to Retain Office until 1967 –
Danang Occupied by Government Forces

Marshal Ky announced at a press conference on May 7 that the

Government would not resign after the general elections, which would be held in September, but would remain in office for at least another year, adding that if an Assembly composed of neutralist and Communist elements were elected he would "struggle against it by every means". He reaffirmed his intention to retain power for at least a year on May 11. The Constituent Assembly, he stated, would draft a Constitution, which would be submitted to a referendum; a Legislative Assembly would then be elected, and would choose a civilian Government. In these statements Marshal Ky in effect repudiated the undertaking given by the Directory on April 14 that the military Government would resign immediately after the election of the Constituent Assembly, which would be empowered to turn itself into a legislative body [see page 95].

At a secret meeting on May 14 the Directory decided to re-establish control over Danang by force, again contrary to its pledge of April 14, the U.S. Embassy in Saigon not being informed of the decision. Two battalions of Marines were secretly flown to Danang during the night, and at 5 a.m. on May 15 launched a surprise attack, supported by tanks and aircraft. The headquarters of the 1st Army Corps, the town hall, and the police headquarters were occupied without resistance.

Fighting, however, broke out during the morning, when the radio station, which had been occupied by the Marines, was retaken by local troops and then recaptured by the Marines after an hour's siege. When the firing died down in the evening the Marines controlled all key installations in the city, but the Tinh Hoi, Pho Da, and Tan Ninh pagodas, with the surrounding districts, were still held by local troops and boy scouts.

Lieut.-General Nguyen Van Thieu (chairman of the Directory) claimed in a broadcast that troops had been sent to Danang after the population and the local troops had risen against the "struggle committee", which had been infiltrated by Communists; this version of events, however, was not supported by any independent source.

Throughout the next three days the situation in Danang remained tense, the Buddhists adopting passive resistance methods; a general strike brought the city to a standstill, and when Government troops advanced on the Tinh Hoi pagoda on May 16 they were stopped by a human wall of

97

praying Buddhists. Local troops took up positions around the pagodas, and on May 17 prevented the Marines from crossing a bridge by threatening to blow it up.

Ngo Trong Anh (State Secretary for Ministerial Co-ordination) resigned from the Government on May 18 as a protest against the attack on Danang. The Buddhist Institute issued a statement accusing the Government of "brazen betrayal of its promises"; demanding the withdrawal of the Government troops from Danang; and calling on their followers to "be ready to act on further orders". Worshippers at the Vien Hoa Dao pagoda, however, were forbidden to organize street demonstrations for the time being.

On May 19 General Huynh Van Cao (commander of the 1st Corps) refused to carry out an order to attack the pagodas and took refuge in the U.S. base at Danang; he was temporarily replaced on the following day by Brigadier-General Do Quoc Dong. Under the command of Colonel Nguyen Ngoc Loan (chief of police and military security) the Government troops surrounded the pagodas on May 19, and exchanges of fire took place between the two sides. Heavy fighting occurred on the following day as the Government forces closed in on the pagodas. The Tan Ninh pagoda was captured on May 21 after a four-hour battle in which a monk was killed and a number of others wounded.

A number of broadcasts by the Viet Cong radio on May 19-20 openly appealed to the rebels to make common cause with the Viet Cong against "the Americans and their lackeys", and offered assistance to the rebel forces in Danang. Thich Tri Quang (the Buddhist leader in Hué), however, alleged on May 21 that these broadcasts came from the Danang base and were intended by the Government to discredit the Buddhist movement.

In a letter addressed to Lieut.-General Lewis Walt (commander of the Marine Force stationed at Danang), the rebel troops appealed to him on May 20 to force the Government to withdraw its troops, and threatened to destroy Danang airfield if he refused to intervene. Mortar shells apparently fired by the rebels landed on the air-base during the fighting on May 21, wounding 11 U.S. servicemen. Buddhist leaders in Danang offered on May 22 to negotiate with the Government commanders if General Walt acted as mediator; the U.S. Embassy, however, stated that it would sponsor peace talks but not mediate them, and General Dong refused to enter into any negotiations.

Armed resistance in Danang ended on May 23, when 400 rebel troops marched out of the Tinh Hoi and Pho Da pagodas and handed over their arms, and the last pocket of resistance in the city was surrounded and occupied on the following day. Dr. Nguyen Van Man was arrested while trying to escape from the Tinh Hoi pagoda and flown to Saigon. Total casualties during the nine days' fighting were reported to be 76 killed and 540 wounded; Buddhist sources, however, put the figure at over 200 killed and nearly 800 wounded.

Buddhist Reactions to Occupation of Danang

Buddhist reactions to the fighting in Danang became increasingly violent after the renewal of the fighting on May 19. An anti-Government demonstration at Mytho (20 miles south of Saigon) was broken up on the same day by police using tear-gas, and in Saigon anti-Government and anti-American demonstrations began on May 20.

When the U.S. Ambassador, Mr. Cabot Lodge, returned to Saigon on May 20 from a visit to Washington, students met him with banners denouncing "Three American infamies in the 20th century—Hiroshima, Dominica, aggression in Danang". After Thich Thien Minh (leader of the Buddhist youth organization) had denounced U.S. military aid for Marshal Ky that evening at a meeting at the Vien Hoa Dao pagoda, about 2,000 people took part in a torchlight demonstration, which the police broke up with tear-gas. Clashes between the police and troops and Buddhist demonstrators subsequently became of daily occurrence in Saigon. Anti-American feeling was increased by an incident on May 23 when a U.S. soldier, whose lorry was surrounded by demonstrators, opened fire and killed a Vietnamese soldier; the crowd then set fire to two U.S. vehicles before being dispersed by troops.

Fire Suicides by Buddhists

A Buddhist nun burned herself to death in Hué on May 29 as a protest against the Government's policies. When the news reached Saigon thousands of Buddhists attempted to march to the centre of the city, but were turned back by troops, who used tear-gas and fired live ammunition over their heads. In the evening a laywoman burned herself to death in the grounds of the Vien Hoa Dao pagoda, and on the following morning a monk similarly committed suicide at Dalat. Thich Tam Chau (president of the Buddhist Institute and leader of its moderate faction) called for an end of ritual suicides on May 30; at a press conference, however, he said that if the Government did not resign "the struggle, including suicides, will continue".

Later the same day a young nun burned herself to death outside the Vien Hoa Dao pagoda, and on May 31 a 17-year-old schoolgirl followed

99

her example in Hué. Following the schoolgirl's death, statements forbidding further suicides were issued in Saigon by Thich Thien Minh and in Hué by Thich Tri Quang, the most prominent leaders of the militant faction among the Buddhists. A nun nevertheless committed suicide in Danang on June 3, and a monk and two nuns in Saigon, Nhatrang, and Quangtri on the following day. The number of fire suicides—nine in seven days—was unprecedented, as was the fact that all but two of the victims were women; six monks and a nun burned themselves to death during the campaign against President Ngo Dinh Diem's regime in 1963, but their deaths were spread over a period of nearly five months [see pages 40, 42].

Enlargement of Directory to Include Civilians — Buddhist Reactions

A "National People's and Armed Forces Political Congress" sponsored by the Government had previously met in Saigon on May 24 to discuss future institutions and the organization of elections; it was attended by over 600 delegates, but was boycotted by the Buddhist Institute and by civil, military, and religious leaders in Hué. Marshal Ky gave an assurance to the congress that elections would be held not later than Sept. 11, and promised to consider a suggestion that the Directory should be enlarged to include civilians.

In an attempt to end the crisis, General Thieu, Marshal Ky, and four other members of the Directory met a Buddhist delegation led by Thich Tam Chau and Thich Thien Minh on May 31 and June 1. The Government announced after the talks that an agreement had been reached whereby 10 civilian members would be added on June 6 to the 10 military members of the Directory, and a "People's and Armed Forces Council" would be established on June 19 to advise the Prime Minister and the Cabinet. Buddhist spokesmen stated that the junta had also agreed to allow the expanded Directory to decide whether to replace General Thieu and to allow the Chief of State to name a new Prime Minister; the Government's communiqué, however, made no reference to the election of a new Chief of State or the possible replacement of Marshal Ky.

The possibility of a compromise between the junta and the Buddhists was greatly weakened when on June 1 Thich Thien Minh was wounded by a grenade which was thrown into his car by terrorists who succeeded in escaping. Buddhist spokesmen alleged that the crime had been committed by Government agents, but other sources suggested that it might have been the work either of Buddhist extremists opposed to the agreement or of Viet Cong agents wishing to prevent a settlement between the Buddhists and the Government.

The Armed Forces Congress (a body of 45 generals and senior commanders) approved on June 6 the addition of 10 civilians to the Directory, but reaffirmed that it remained "the responsibility of the armed forces" to lead the country for the present.

The new members of the Directory, who included representatives of the four main religious communities, were described by *The New York Times* as "ageing 'intellectual politicians', a body of generally conservative, earnest men who had come and gone often in public life, leaving behind no great personal following or reputation".

The Buddhist Institute stated in a communiqué issued on the same day that the addition of civilians to the Directory would not solve any problem unless Marshal Ky and General Thieu were removed from office.

Conflict between Moderate and Militant Buddhist Factions

The agreement with the Government and the attack on Thich Thien Minh brought to a head the division inside the Buddhist movement between the moderate and militant factions. At a meeting at the Vien Hoa Dao pagoda, Thich Ho Giac (usually regarded as a militant) appealed for the suspension of demonstrations until June 6, when the struggle would be resumed if the Government did not carry out its promises. A number of monks thereupon poured petrol over their robes and threatened to burn themselves as a protest against the negotiations with the Government, but were overpowered by boy scouts and carried bodily from the hall.

In a communiqué issued on June 2 Thich Tam Chau stated that General Thieu and Marshal Ky had "promised to be ready to hand over power to other persons after the Committee for the Direction of the State has been reorganized on June 6", and again appealed for the suspension of demonstrations. Marshal Ky, however, denied on the same day that he was prepared to resign, and further anti-Government demonstrations took place in the evening. Thich Tam Chau accordingly tendered his resignation as president of the Buddhist Institute on June 3, stating that he had failed in his mission, but the council of the Institute decided the following day not to accept it. A Buddhist spokesman stated on June 5 that the Institute would not co-operate with the enlarged Directory and would refuse to nominate any representatives to it, as the real issue remained the resignation of General Thieu and Marshal Ky.

The council of the Buddhist Institute decided on June 7 to disband the "Struggle Movement Committee" headed by Thich Thien Minh, and instead to set up a "Committee for the Protection of Buddhism" under the leadership of Thich Tam Chau. This decision was regarded as a victory for the moderate policy advocated by the latter, who again urged the suspension of all street demonstrations and the ending of fire suicides; he told a crowd of 5,000 Buddhists, however, that he would order a "non-co-operation campaign" if Marshal Ky and General Thieu did not resign soon. The Buddhist Institute announced on June 11 that it would boycott the general elections if they were arranged by the present Government.

The dissensions inside the Buddhist leadership continued during July. The council of the Buddhist Institute on July 13 called on Thich Tam Chau to take firmer action or resign, whereupon Thich Tam Chau, who was staying away from the council's meetings, nominally for health reasons, said that he would retire from his duties for two months. In a letter of Aug. 2 to Marshal Ky and General Thieu, the council accused them of oppressing and deceiving the people in order to retain power, and challenged them to bring the Buddhist leaders to trial.

Differences among Buddhist Leaders

The succession of political defeats suffered by the United Buddhist Church since the occupation of Danang by Government troops in May led to profound differences among its leaders. Thich Tri Quang, leader of the militant faction, ended on Sept. 16 the hunger strike which he had begun on June 8, but reaffirmed his complete opposition to the Government's policies. Thich Tam Chau, leader of the moderate faction, on the other hand, appealed to his supporters on Sept. 17 to suspend their campaign against the Government. As they were unable to reach agreement on their policy, the directing committee of the Buddhist Secular Institute (Vien Hoa Dao) submitted their resignation on Oct. 14 to Thich Tinh Khiet, the head of the Church.

102

At a general assembly of monks and nuns which met on Oct. 21 so many clashes occurred between the rival factions that Thich Tinh Khiet dissolved it on the following day. The assembly nevertheless continued its session in defiance of this order, and decided on Oct. 23 to remove both Thich Tam Chau from his post as director of the Vien Hoa Dao and Thich Tri Quang from the post of general secretary of the Higher Council of the Buddhist Order, and to replace Thich Tam Chau by Thich Tien Hoa, who had attempted to act as a mediator between the two factions. Thich Tam Chau, however, denied that his dismissal was valid, and installed himself in the Vien Hoa Dao pagoda under the protection of his supporters.

Agitation against New Statute for Buddhist Church

After a period of political inactivity, the United Buddhist Church became increasingly involved again in the summer of 1967. Thich Tinh Khiet, the head of the Buddhist Church, appealed to General Thieu and President Ho Chi Minh on March 20 to order a truce in military operations on May 23, the anniversary of the birth of the Buddha. A 20-year-old nun publicly burned herself to death in Saigon on May 16 as a gesture of support for this appeal; this was the first fire suicide which had taken place since June 1966.

A new statute for the United Buddhist Church published on July 18 virtually gave control of the Church to the pro-Government faction led by Thich Tam Chau, although the militant faction was supported by the majority of members of the Church and had previously held 20 of the 25 seats on its governing body. Thich Tinh Khiet sent letters of protest against the Government's action on Aug. 24 to Pope Paul VI and U Thant, the U.N. Secretary-General. From Sept. 24 the militants intensified their agitation against the statute, which they co-ordinated with that against the validation of the presidential election [see pages 123-132].

Several hundred monks took part in a protest march to the presidential palace in Saigon on Sept. 28. At an interview with Thich Tri Quang, leader of the militant faction, General Thieu refused to revise the statute until the two factions reached agreement among themselves, whereupon Thich Tri Quang and other monks began a sit-down strike outside the palace. He announced on Oct. 3 that 110 monks and nuns had volunteered to burn themselves alive if the Government rejected their claims; a nun committed fire suicide at Cantho on the same day, another at Sadec on Oct. 8 and a third in Saigon on Oct. 22. Thich Tri Quang, who had been on hunger strike since Oct. 5, abandoned his vigil on Oct. 10 on Thich Tinh Khiet's orders, whilst stating that he would begin it again if the militants did not obtain satisfaction.

The Directory again refused on Oct. 24 to suspend the statute until the two factions had reached agreement; in reply the militants refused to open negotiations with Thich Tam Chau's faction. A monk burned himself alive at Quang Ngai on Oct. 31, and a nun at Nhatrang on the following day. Thich Tinh Khiet announced on Nov. 1 that he was prepared to commit suicide if the Government did not withdraw the statute.

Anti-American Riots in Hué — City Occupied by Government Troops — Disciplinary Measures against Rebel Generals

The situation in Hué remained tense during the summer of 1966. The garrison, commanded by General Phan Xuan Nhuan, fully supported the Buddhists; Lieut.-General Nguyen Chanh Thi, whose removal from the command of the 1st Corps in March had initiated the crisis, remained in the city, and had been joined there after the attack on Danang by General Ton That Dinh. After the fall of Danang, the Government established an economic blockade of Hué; supplies of fuel and raw materials were cut off, forcing factories to close, the garrison remained unpaid, and even the hospitals were refused medical supplies.

The funeral on May 26 of an officer shot by an American on May 17 [during a visit by General Huynh Van Cao to Hué] developed into an anti-American demonstration, led by Thich Tri Quang; over 6,000 people took part in the funeral procession, including 200 soldiers of the 1st Division in uniform. While it was in progress students sacked and burned the U.S. Information Service library and cinema, without interference from the police, and warned the U.S. Vice-Consul that they would take "stronger action" unless President Johnson intervened in the conflict between the Government and the Buddhists. Officials evacuated the Consulate on the following day and moved into the heavily defended compound housing U.S. military advisers.

In an attempt to re-establish the Government's authority, the pro-Government major, Lieut.-Colonel Phan Van Khoa, ordered on May 30 the withdrawal from Hué of all but a token force of the 1st Division. In obedience to an ultimatum from Colonel Khoa, Buddhist students

104

evacuated the radio station, which they had controlled since March, on the following day. Major-General Hoang Xuan Lam was appointed to the command of the 1st Corps on June 1—the fifth officer to hold the post in less than three months.

Violent rioting flared up again on June 1, when students sacked and burned the U.S. Consulate and Colonel Khoa's house, neither the garrison nor the police making any attempt to intervene. Troops of the 1st Division, including armoured units, moved into the city on the following day, but it was disputed which side they were supporting. On June 5 Colonel Khoa dismissed the city's chief of police for co-operating with the rebels, and an order was issued banning anti-Government and anti-American demonstrations and providing for the conscription of students arrested for demonstrating.

The Buddhists replied to these measures on June 6 by launching a passive resistance campaign. A general strike closed all the shops and 80 per cent of the Government offices, and thousands of household shrines were used to build barricades, blocking all the main roads into the city. Similar barricades were constructed in Danang and Qui Nhon, where the road leading to the U.S. military port area was cut. After the blocking of the roads had forced the Government and U.S. troops to abandon an operation against the Viet Cong, however, Thich Tri Quang ordered the shrines to be removed from the main coastal highway on June 9. He had begun an unlimited fast as a protest against the Government's policy on the previous day, and after 44 hours without food was taken to hospital on June 10.

Three battalions of Government troops were flown from Danang to a camp near Hué on June 7, but made no immediate move against the city. On June 10, however, 400 riot police entered Hué, occupied the police headquarters, and began disarming and purging the local police, whilst on June 13 another 120 riot police arrived. On June 16 a parachute battalion entered the city and began removing the shrines from the streets; troops of the 1st Division withdrew into the citadel without attempting to resist, but two civilians were killed in clashes with the Government troops. On the following day a second parachute battalion arrived, and Colonel Khoa proclaimed martial law and imposed a 24-hour curfew. Two additional battalions of Marines and police were flown to Hué in U.S. aircraft, raising the strength of the Government forces to about 3,000 men: the citadel was occupied without opposition, the garrison apparently having withdrawn secretly, and on June 19 Government troops took over the last area of the city still in rebel hands.

General Nhuan was deprived of command of the 1st Infantry Division on June 18 and succeeded by Colonel Ngo Quang Truong. Thich Tri Quang was arrested on June 20 and flown on the following day to Saigon, where he was detained in a clinic. On June 22 troops occupied Quangtri, the only remaining centre of Buddhist opposition in Central Vietnam, and cleared the streets of barricades of shrines which had been erected there two days before.

Four successive commanders of the 1st Corps—Generals Nguyen Chanh Thi, Nguyen Van Chuan, Ton That Dinh, and Huynh Van Cao—appeared before a disciplinary tribunal on July 9, together with General Nhuan. General Dinh was cashiered, and the other four permitted to retire from the Army; General Nhuan was retired with the rank of colonel, which reduced his pension. They were also sentenced to 60 days' detention, which General Thi and General Dinh would serve in prison and the others under house arrest. Before completing his sentence, General Thi was allowed to leave on July 31 for voluntary exile in the U.S.A., officially for health reasons.

Buddhist Demonstrations in Saigon — Vien Hoa Dao Pagoda Occupied by Police

As a protest against the Government's pressure on Hué, Buddhist demonstrations began again in Saigon on June 12 and barricades of altars were erected in the streets; Thich Tam Chau, however, ordered their removal on the following day.

During a demonstration on June 14 a man believed to be a security agent shot and wounded three Buddhists who attacked him; a rumour spread that they had been shot by an American, whereupon the crowd burned a U.S. military jeep. Police fired over the heads of the rioters, seriously wounding a girl, and threw tear-gas shells into the Vien Hoa Dao pagoda. The council of the Buddhist Institute afterwards overruled Thich Tam Chau's order forbidding demonstrations, and called for altars to be used as road-blocks. In repeated clashes with the police, a man was killed and eight others were wounded on June 15, and a young nun was seriously wounded the following day.

After a policeman had been killed on June 18, the police erected barbed-wire barricades round the Vien Hoa Dao pagoda in an attempt to starve the monks into surrendering a youth alleged to have killed him. While the blockade of the pagoda continued, Marshal Ky wrote to Thich Tam Chau on June 21 disclaiming any intention of repressing Buddhism, and promising to pay compensation to the families of those killed in Danang and to repair damage to pagodas there. In reply, Thich Tam Chau demanded an assurance of the safety of Thich Tri Quang and other monks and nuns who had taken part in the anti-Government struggle; the ending of the blockade of the Vien Hoa Dao pagoda; and the release of all persons arrested for political reasons since March.

The police allowed 200 Buddhists to leave the Vien Hoa Dao pagoda on June 22, but about 400 monks and laymen remained inside the building. On the following day troops and police stormed the pagoda and arrested the occupants, including the youth alleged to have killed the policeman.

On June 24 Thich Tam Chau strongly protested to Marshal Ky against the occupation of the pagoda, which, he said, "heavily hurts the dignity of the United Buddhist Church". Marshal Ky expressed regret for the action of the police in a letter of June 30 to Thich Tam Chau, but contended that the Government had been obliged to ensure the safety and freedom of the Buddhist leaders, who had been under pressure from extremists; he gave assurances that all persons arrested during the recent demonstrations would be released, except those connected with the Viet Cong, and that compensation would be paid to those injured and for the damage to the pagodas. 283 monks, nuns and Buddhist laymen were subsequently released on July 4.

Thich Nhat Hanh's Statement on Buddhist Aims

Thich Nhat Hanh, director of the Institute of Social Studies of the Buddhist University of Saigon, made a tour of the United States, Britain, Scandinavia, and France in June and July, during which he was received by Mr. McNamara (then U.S. Defence Secretary) and gave a series of press conferences at which he defined the Buddhists' political aims. He made the following statement in Paris on July 1:

"The Buddhists' action ... represents the mobilization of the nationalist forces which do not form part of the Liberation Front against a Government which appears simply as an extension of U.S. foreign policy. The immediate objective of this action is the establishment of an independent civilian Government. Its motive is an intense desire for peace. The Buddhists do not seek political power for themselves, but are working for a civilian Government in which all religious groups will be represented. ...

"Every day the war continues the Front wins more support from the peasants. The essential element of this war is not military but psychological. The United States, the most powerful nation on earth, can probably win a military victory, but only at the price of the destruction of the whole country and its people. If, however, the United States decided really to seek for peace, made it obvious that it was doing so, and undertook to go once peace was established, the National Liberation Front would lose a great part of its arguments. The Front is aware of the fact. It could not refuse to co-operate if the United States made a real effort for peace. ...

107

"The Buddhists do not accept the argument that there is no other choice than victory or surrender. Another possibility would be offered by a combination of the following initiatives: an end of bombing in the North and the South, an end of all offensive military action by the Americans, and the formation of an independent non-military Government. As it would be physically impossible to withdraw all U.S. forces immediately, such a proposal would not be politically realistic. However, a solemn engagement to withdraw the U.S. troops at a specified date, after a limited period, might be made convincing by a U.S. initiative on a significant scale. The 37-day pause in the raids on North Vietnam in December and January, despite the publicity on the subject, was not a step of this kind, as it was accompanied by the arrival of U.S. reinforcements. The South Vietnamese do not believe that the Americans mean to leave. How can Hanoi and the Front believe it?

"We share the view that the Front must take part in negotiations, since it is taking part in the war. But so must a legitimate, representative, independent South Vietnamese Government. Negotiations must deal with Vietnam's difficulties, and it is for the Vietnamese to negotiate. A promise must be made to respect the Geneva Agreements. In particular, this would lead up to the withdrawal of foreign troops from their bases after, say, eight or 10 months. . . .

"Of course, the North Vietnamese must also withdraw their troops. . . . But during my tour I am not emphasizing that problem. . . . For many Westerners it is tempting to free themselves from a guilt complex about America's actions by claiming that Washington intervened because of a North Vietnamese invasion. There was no serious infiltration from the North before U.S. domination over the South had become a reality and the Saigon Government had refused to hold the promised elections. There are North Vietnamese in the South; I want them to go, but the principal reason for their intervention was U.S. intervention, which took place first. . . ."

Formation of People's and Armed Forces Council — Cabinet Changes

The People's and Armed Forces Council was officially installed on July 5, with powers to advise the Prime Minister on economic, cultural, social, and other problems of internal policy. Its 80 members included 20 officers, 18 members of the Electoral Law Commission, professional men, businessmen, and representatives of the Montagnard and Cambodian communities.

Marshal Ky carried out a Cabinet reshuffle on July 13, whereby *inter alia* the Ministry of the Interior was abolished and control of the police transferred to a new Ministry of Security. A feature of the reorganization was the appointment of a civilian Second Deputy Premier in the person of Dr. Nguyen Luu Vien, a physician at the *Institut Pasteur* who served as Minister of the Interior in two previous Governments and who is a member of a relatively non-political Buddhist sect. The other Deputy Premier was the Minister of Defence.

108

IX. CONSTITUTIONAL DEVELOPMENTS – PRESIDENTIAL AND LEGISLATIVE ELECTIONS

Adoption of Electoral Law

A committee of 32 members, consisting of representatives of provincial and municipal councils, delegates from the Buddhist, Roman Catholic, Caodaist and Hoa Hao Churches jurists, and politicians, was appointed on May 5 to draft an electoral law, and submitted its report to the Directory on June 7. The report proposed that the Constituent Assembly should exercise legislative powers, but this proposal was rejected by the Directory.

A decree on the procedure of the Assembly, which was issued on June 19, provided that it should submit the draft Constitution within six months from its first meeting to the chairman of the Directory, who would promulgate it within 30 days. During this period he might propose amendments to the Constitution, which would be automatically adopted unless rejected by a majority of two-thirds of the total number of deputies. The Assembly would be dissolved when the Constitution was promulgated, and the Directory would be responsible for setting up the national institutions stipulated in the Constitution within three to six months from its promulgation.

A decree on electoral procedure was also issued on June 19, its provisions being as follows:

(1) Elections to the Constituent Assembly would take place on September 11.

(2) The Assembly would consist of 117 deputies. There would be one deputy for every 50,000 voters in each prefecture, province, and provincial capital; if in addition to the multiple of 50,000 the remainder exceeded 30,000 the constituency would have an additional deputy. Any province or provincial capital with less than 50,000 voters would have one deputy.

(3) Each province and town would be a single constituency, returning from one to four members. Saigon, however, would be divided into three constituencies, returning a total of 16 members, and the adjoining province of Gia Dinh into two constituencies, returning five members each.

(4) Four seats would be reserved for Vietnamese citizens of Cambodian descent and nine for Montagnards. The Montagnard representatives would be chosen in accordance with tribal custom.

(5) All Vietnamese citizens over 18 would be entitled to vote.

(6) Candidates must be Vietnamese citizens and at least 25. Persons who had been convicted of a serious offence, had been deprived of their civil rights, had disobeyed military draft orders, or had been "directly or indirectly working for the Communists or pro-Communist neutralists or involved in activities advantageous to the Communists", as well as civil servants or military personnel who had been dismissed for disciplinary reasons, would be ineligible as candidates.

(7) In constituencies with more than one seat (except those with two seats one of which was reserved for Vietnamese of Cambodian descent) lists of candidates equal to the number of seats would be put forward. Each list would include a number of alternate candidates.

(8) In each constituency a council would be established to decide whether the candidates were eligible. If a candidate was eliminated as a Communist or neutralist the list on which he appeared would not be allowed to run for election; in other cases an eliminated candidate would be replaced by an alternate. Appeals might be submitted to a central council in Saigon, whose decision would be final.

(9) In single-member constituencies the candidate with the largest vote would be returned. In other constituencies seats would be distributed by proportional representation.

Election of Constituent Assembly in September 1966

Elections to the Constituent Assembly were held on Sept. 11 in the areas of South Vietnam under Government control. The main interest of the elections centred on the size of the vote rather than on the candidates returned, in view of the fact that both the National Liberation Front (the so-called Viet Cong) and the United Buddhist Church had called for a boycott of the elections.

The 117 seats were contested by 540 candidates. 735 candidates had been nominated, but 59 of these were refused permission to stand for political reasons, whilst 136 others were either eliminated on technical grounds or withdrew their nominations, some on the ground that they had been subjected to "pressure". Most candidates were largely unknown; the chief exceptions were Phan Khac Suu (Chief of State in 1964-65), Tran Van Van (chairman of the People's and Armed Forces Council) and Dr. Dang Van Sung (a newspaper editor and leading member of the right-wing Dai-Viet party), all of whom were elected in Saigon.

The programmes of the electoral lists contained no reference to the form to be taken by the Constitution, the only issue on which the Assembly was qualified to decide.

Le Monde commented that at election meetings "the discussion does not deal with the problem of the choice between a presidential and a parliamentary regime. Without its being necessary to say so, the question is already settled in most people's minds. The Government wants a presidential regime and will get it."

The United Buddhist Church urged voters to boycott the elections, and was supported in its appeal by a number of representatives of the Roman Catholic, Caodaist, Hoa Hao, and Protestant communities. Buddhist monks staged a demonstration against the elections in Saigon on Sept. 9, during which 11 of them were arrested, and nearly 500 monks and nuns began a three-day fast on the same day in the An Quan pagoda.

The Viet Cong denounced the elections as a "farce" and the secret radio of the National Liberation Front, according to *Le Monde,* broadcast veiled threats against those standing as candidates and against electors who intended to cast their votes, saying that their safety "could not be guaranteed". *Le Monde* also stated that in certain areas controlled by the Viet Cong its political agents had told the population not to apply for the election cards required for voting, while in others they confiscated people's identity cards to prevent them from obtaining election cards. The Government nevertheless announced at the beginning of September that 5,289,652 persons, or about two-thirds of the eligible electorate, had registered on the electoral rolls.

Although it had been feared that the Viet Cong would seek to sabotage the election campaign by terrorist methods, the number of acts of terrorism reported in August was actually smaller than in July. There was a marked increase in terrorism immediately before and during the voting, however. The Army and police were authorized to shoot at sight anyone

111

seeking to interfere with the conduct of the elections; a man who tore down a Government poster urging people to vote was shot dead by the police in Saigon on Aug. 31.

On the eve of the elections the Government launched an anti-French campaign, accusing Frenchmen of plotting to "sabotage" the elections. Two influential French businessmen were arrested in Saigon on Sept. 7 on a charge of giving 50,000,000 piastres [a sum almost equal to the Government's entire expenditure on the elections] to religious and political groups opposed to the elections, and were detained until Sept. 20.

According to official figures issued late on Sept. 11, votes cast were 4,274,812 out of the total registered electorate of 5,289,652, a poll of 80.8 per cent. It was stated that the proportion of voters was highest in Phy Bon province, in Central Vietnam (97.5 per cent), and lowest in Saigon (66 per cent), and that the figures in the Buddhist strongholds of Hué and Danang had been 85 and 81 per cent respectively. *The New York Times* stated that "foreign observers who roamed freely on election day generally agreed there were few irregularities".

At a press conference on Sept. 17 the Prime Minister, Air Vice-Marshal Nguyen Cao Ky, declared that the results were "a vote of no confidence in the Viet Cong" and that "their claims to exercise control and influence over important sectors of the population have been unmasked as lies". The Viet Cong radio, on the other hand, ridiculed the elections as a fraud built upon "concocted, phoney figures", claiming that the entire population of the area under Government control was less than 4,000,000. The United Buddhist Church similarly alleged that less than half the population had voted and that the official figures were "fraudulent".

In Washington, where Government spokesmen had previously said that a 50 per cent vote must be regarded as very successful, President Johnson's press secretary, Mr. Bill Moyers, stated on Sept. 12: "We are heartened by the fact that the elections were held, and heartened by the size of the heavy turn-out as reported."

Among Western press comments, *The Times* said that "as a test of Government control over that portion of the population which it claims to control and as a test of administrative efficiency, the election was unquestionably a victory", but in another dispatch it stated that "the high turn-out in the 1st Corps area where the Buddhist cities of Danang and Hué are situated, contrasts rather markedly with the Saigon figure of 66 per cent, suggesting strong local pressure and some inflation of returns".

The New York Times wrote: "Many South Vietnamese, it was acknowledged, undoubtedly went to the polls not out of choice but because of a desire not to offend village chiefs carrying out the Government's orders for a large turn-out. . . . To a certain degree the unexpectedly large turn-out of registered voters was viewed as an expression of popular will for replacing the present military junta with a constitutional, representative Government. In the area of Buddhist-dominated Hué, for example, where there was a heavy turn-out, many voters, it was thought, went to the polls not because of sympathy for or pressure by the Government, but to show their desire for a new form of government. . . ".

A correspondent who witnessed the elections in the Mekong delta wrote in *Le Monde:* "Of the hundreds of peasants who dropped into the ballot box the photograph of the candidate of their choice, only a handful had any idea what it was all about. . . . There is scarcely any doubt that many electors thought it better to vote in order to keep on the right side of the local authorities. . . . Between the threat of reprisals from the Viet Cong and reprisals from the Government, they have chosen the Government. . . ".

The Constituent Assembly met for its first session in Saigon on Sept. 27. Phan Khac Suu was elected president of the Assembly on Oct. 26, receiving 61 votes against 44 for Tran Dien and nine for Nguyen Ba Luong, the oldest member of the Assembly.

Meanwhile, an indication of the *détente* between the Government and the Buddhists had been given by the release on Oct. 1 of the 11 monks arrested on Sept. 9 and the solemn re-installation of the Buddhist hierarchy in the Buddhist Institute which it had left several months earlier.

National Liberation Front's Proposal for Coalition Government

The North Vietnamese press agency released on Sept. 28 the text of an interview granted to Mr. Wilfred Burchett, an Australian journalist, on Aug. 28 by Nguyen Huu Tho, president of the National Liberation Front, in which he proposed the formation of a broadly-based coalition Government and re-defined the Front's conditions for a peace settlement.

Nguyen Huu Tho said that the Front's aim was to form "a broad and democratic coalition Government consisting of representatives of all social strate, nationalities, religions communities and patriotic groups", and expressed the opinion that "there are great possibilities for broadening co-operation with the other organizations, forces and personalities in South Vietnam, regardless of their former activities". The Front, he stated, was prepared to co-operate even with those who had participated in the Ngo Dinh Diem regime and succeeding Governments, provided only that they would agree to "win back national sovereignty, realize the right to freedom and democracy, put an end to the U.S. policy of intervention and aggression, and achieve peace and neutrality in South Vietnam". They would refuse to co-operate with "a handful of traitors" such as Lieut.-General Nguyen Van Thieu (the South Vietnamese Chief of State) and Marshal Ky.

113

Nguyen Huu Tho defined the Front's peace terms as follows:

"(1) The United States must end the war of aggression in South Vietnam, withdraw the troops and weapons of the United States and its satellites from South Vietnam and dissolve all U.S. military bases there.

(2) The United States must respect the national rights of the South Vietnamese people, which are independence, democracy, peace and neutrality. The internal affairs of South Vietnam must be settled by the South Vietnamese people themselves without foreign interference. The reunification of Vietnam must be decided by the people of both zones of Vietnam.

(3) The South Vietnamese National Liberation Front, the only genuine representative of the South Vietnamese people, must have its decisive place and make its voice heard in any political solution concerning South Vietnam."

It was commented in the foreign Press that Nguyen Huu Tho had not demanded that the withdrawal of the U.S. forces from South Vietnam should be a precondition for peace negotiations.

Cabinet Crisis

A serious Cabinet crisis developed in October, as a result partly of rivalries between the Ministers who came from South Vietnam and those who were exiles from North Vietnam, and partly of the civilian Ministers' resentment of the military junta's high-handed methods. Marshal Ky and the majority of the junta were North Vietnamese, as were Brigadier-General Nguyen Ngoc Loan (the Director of National Police, who had taken a leading part in the suppression of the Buddhist revolt at Danang) and many influential civilian officials.

The crisis originated when Dr. Nguyen Tan Loc (the Secretary of State for Health), who had demoted some North Vietnamese officials in favour of Southerners, was arrested on Sept. 29 by General Loan's order on a charge of "Southern separatist manoeuvres". Through Marshal Ky's intervention he was released on the following day, whereupon he accused Dr. Nguyen Ba Kha (the Health Minister), a North Vietnamese, of procuring his arrest. Dr. Kha subsequently resigned on Oct. 4 and was replaced by Dr. Tran Lu Y.

Six Ministers had meanwhile sent a joint letter of resignation to Marshal Ky on Oct. 2, protesting against "regional discrimination" and "police State" methods and demanding General Loan's dismissal as an assurance against "any return to a police regime". The letter was signed by Dr. Nguyen Luu Vien (Second Deputy Premier), Nguyen Van Truong (Education), Truong Van Thuan (Transport), Tran Ngoc Lieng (Social

114

Affairs), Vo Long Trieu (Youth), and Nguyen Huu Hung (Labour), the last-named being the only Northerner in the group. Talks between Marshal Ky and the six Ministers produced no result, as the former refused to take any action against General Loan. Au Truong Thanh (Minister for the Economy and Finance), who had just returned from a visit to Washington, informed Marshal Ky on Oct. 16 that he too would resign if the crisis was not quickly and satisfactorily settled, and stated that he was disheartened "to realize that the security of high-ranking members of the Government is not at all guaranteed, and that threatening arrest was again motivated by the spirit of regional discrimination". A temporary settlement was reached on Oct. 19 when Truong Van Thuan and Nguyen Huu Hung withdrew their resignations, and the other five Ministers agreed to remain in office until after the forthcoming conference in Manila between the South Vietnamese Government and its allies. On Nov. 11, 1966, however, Marshal Nguyen Cao Ky announced the resignation of Nguyen Van Truong, Tran Ngoc Lieng and Vo Long Trieu.

Cabinet changes were announced on Nov. 18 under which three newcomers, all from South Vietnam, entered the Government, a Department for Cultural Affairs was set up, and the Ministry of the Economy was divided into separate Ministries of Industry and Commerce. The former Minister for the Economy, Au Truong Thanh, was dropped from the Cabinet.

Assassination of Tran Van Van

Tran Van Van, a prominent member of the Constituent Assembly and former chairman of the People's and Armed Forces Council, was shot dead in Saigon on Dec. 7, 1966, by a youth riding on the pillion of a motor-cycle which overtook Tran Van Van's car as he was driving to the Assembly. The motor-cycle was afterwards stopped and one of the youths arrested, the other escaping. The arrested man, Vo Van En, who was produced by the police at a press conference the same evening, said that he had been trained by the Viet Cong for a month to assassinate Tran Van Van and had been sent to Saigon a week before the murder to learn riding a motor-cycle; though unrepentant and saying that he was ready to die if he was sentenced, he claimed, however, that he had driven the motor-cycle and that the shots had been fired by his pillion passenger.

115

The *Guardian* correspondent in Saigon commented: "The choice of Tran Van Van by the Viet Cong for assassination is particularly astute, because had not the culprit been apprehended the murder would have been used in political quarters here to sow further discord between the northerners and southerners in the Government.

"Tran Van Van was passionately devoted to the southern cause and was believed to have been deeply involved in the action of eight southern Ministers in resigning from the Government just before the Manila conference in an attempt to force the Prime Minister, Air Vice-Marshal Ky, to dismiss his northern police chief. Although he did not ally himself to any bloc in the Constituent Assembly, he was known as being opposed to the Government on the issue of the number of northerners in it."

Vo Van En was sentenced to death on Jan 10, 1967. In a letter to General Thieu, Tran Van Van's widow subsequently questioned his guilt and asked that he should be pardoned "in order to avoid a new crime".

In her letter she wrote: "Vo Van En is only a pawn in this crime. The Viet Cong would have been stupid to choose a half-blind man, whose pock-marked face made it easy for the police to find him, to carry it out. Before his death my husband was fully aware that as he was opposed to the Government he was in imminent danger and death was inevitable." He had told his friends, the letter continued, that he feared assassination because of his opposition to the decree authorizing the Directory to veto the Constitution.

Marshal Ky's Statements on Policy during His Visit to Australia

Air Vice-Marshal Nguyen Cao Ky, accompanied by his wife, arrived in Canberra on Jan. 18, 1967, for a four-day visit to Australia.

At a televised press conference after his arrival Marshal Ky declared that South Vietnam did not want to invade the North, nor was it opposed to negotiations. "At the present time" he would accept a settlement short of victory, dividing the country at the 17th parallel and allowing North Vietnam to remain Communist, but one day South Vietnam would "defeat the aggressors and unify our country".

On the following day Air Vice-Marshal Ky, speaking on the aims of his Government, said: "We are not fighting for territory which is not ours. . . , not for an alien cause or ideology. . . , not to keep any group in power. This is not a civil war, for not even the most articulate critics of our Administration have joined the Viet Cong. We are fighting for . . . the right to be left alone, the right to grow and develop in the way we choose, the right to give our people freely the chance to select the Government."

Dismissal of General Nguyen Huu Co

The Deputy Premier and Defence Minister, Lieut.-General Nguyen Huu Co, left Saigon on Jan. 17 for an official visit to Formosa; it was suggested in the foreign Press that the object of his mission was to prevent him from

116

seizing power during Marshal Ky's absence. A cable was sent to him on Jan. 22 ordering him not to return to Saigon, and special security measures were adopted on the following day; all aircraft arriving from Formosa and Hong Kong were searched to ensure that he had not returned, between 30 and 40 officers closely associated with him were placed under house arrest or posted outside Saigon, and Marshal Ky's residence and the Air Force staff headquarters were guarded by police. The Security Minister, Major-General Linh Quang Vien, met General Co in Hong Kong on Jan. 25, and informed him that if he returned he would be tried by court martial for corruption. General Co was the last prominent South Vietnamese member of the ruling military junta.

A communiqué issued on Jan. 27 announced that Lieut.-General Cao Van Vien had been appointed Defence Minister *vice* General Co, and would also retain the post of Chief of General Staff.

The New Constitution, 1967

The Constituent Assembly took its first major decision on the form of the new Constitution on Dec. 15, 1966, when after 10 days of debate it voted in favour of government by a popularly-elected President assisted by a Prime Minister. This was followed, on Dec. 20, by a vote in favour of popular election of province chiefs and mayors, who in the past had been appointed by the Government; it was agreed, however, that the Government might dismiss them if they violated the Constitution, the law or national policy. On the following day the Assembly decided by 87 votes to 14 that the Legislature should consist of two Houses. After the Assembly had agreed on the main principles of the new Constitution, its drafting was entrusted to a committee, which completed its work on Jan. 10, 1967. The clauses were then voted on individually by the Assembly, and a number of amendments introduced.

The Directory and the Cabinet, at a joint meeting on March 19, decided to approve the Constitution without amendment. Foreign commentators suggested that General Thieu and the Prime Minister, Air Vice-Marshal Nguyen Cao Ky, who were to leave on the following day for talks with President Johnson in Guam, had decided to accept the Constitution as it stood because they wished to present the President with evidence of some

117

progress towards democratic government. Final approval was given to the Constitution on March 27 by the Congress of the Armed Forces, to which under the Provisional Charter the Directory was responsible. The majority of the Congress at first voted against acceptance, and objected in particular to the absence of a balance of powers between the Executive, the Legislature and the Judiciary and the assumption of legislative powers by the Constituent Assembly; after General Thieu and Marshal Ky had appealed to the Congress to reconsider its decision, however, it voted in favour of adoption by 25 votes to eight, with two abstentions.

The Constitution was formally promulgated by General Thieu at a public ceremony on April 1, in the presence of members of the Assembly, the diplomatic corps, and representatives of religious and other organizations and the national minorities; most of the Buddhist organizations boycotted the ceremony, however. On the previous day 3,000 Roman Catholics had demonstrated in protest against the omission of any reference to God from the preamble to the Constitution.

The Constitution

A detailed summary of the new Constitution, which consisted of a Preamble and 117 Articles, is given below, listing the principal provisions.

Preamble

The preamble stated that the Assembly had approved the Constitution, "conscious that after many years of foreign domination, followed by the partition of the national territory, dictatorship and war, the people of Vietnam must take responsibility before history, to perpetuate their self-reliant spirit and at the same time to welcome progressive ideas in order to establish a republican form of government of the people, by the people and for the people, for the purpose of uniting the nation, unifying the territory and assuring independence, freedom and democracy with justice and altruism for the present and future generations".

I. Basic Provisions

Vietnam was an independent, unified and territorially indivisible republic, in which sovereignty resided in the whole people. The State recognized and guaranteed the basic rights of every citizen, including equality of all citizens without discrimination as to sex, religion, race or political party, and would give special support to "minority compatriots". The functions and powers of the legislative, executive and judicial branches of government must be clearly delineated, and their activities co-ordinated in order to realize social order and prosperity on the basis of freedom, democracy and social justice. The Republic opposed Communism in any form, and every activity designed to publicize or carry out Communism was

118

prohibited. Vietnam would comply with those provisions of international law which were not contrary to its national sovereignty and the principle of equality between nations; would oppose all forms of aggression; and strive to contribute to the building of international peace and security.

II. Rights and Duties of Citizens

No one might be arrested or detained without a legal order, except *in flagrante delicto*, or tortured, threatened or forced to confess, and a confession so obtained would not be considered valid evidence. A defendant was entitled to a speedy and public trial; had the right to a defence lawyer in every phase of the interrogation; and would be considered innocent until found guilty. A person unjustly detained had the right to demand compensation from the State.

The Constitution also recognized the inviolability of domicile; privacy of correspondence; freedom of religious belief and freedom to preach and practise religion, as long as there was no harm to public order and morality, though no religion would be recognized as the State religion; freedom of speech and of the Press, as long as it did not harm personal honour, national security and good morals; the right of assembly and the right to form associations; the right to vote, run for office and participate in public affairs; and the right to engage in overt, non-violent and legal opposition. Censorship would be confined to films and the theatre. Basic education was free and compulsory, and talented persons without means would be given support to continue their studies.

Every citizen had the right and duty to work, and the State would endeavour to create employment for all citizens. Freedom to join trade unions and to strike was respected within the framework of the law. It was the duty of the State to establish a system of social security and public health.

The State guaranteed the right to private property, and advocated a policy of making the people property-owners. Expropriation or requisition by the State for the common good must be accompanied by speedy and just compensation. Freedom of enterprise and competition was recognized, but might not be exercised to secure monopoly or control of the market. The State encouraged and assisted economic co-operation, gave special support to those who had a low standard of living, advocated raising the living standard of rural citizens and would help farmers to have land for cultivation. Workers had the right to choose representatives to participate in the management of business enterprises, especially in matters concerning wages and working conditions.

Military personnel elected to public office or serving in the Central Government must be demobilized or take unpaid leave of absence. Military personnel on active service might not engage in political party activity.

The State respected the customs of the racial minorities and would establish special courts to deal with cases involving their customs.

Every citizen had the duty to defend the Republic; to defend the Constitution and respect the law; to fulfill his military obligations; and to pay taxes.

Any restriction upon the basic rights of citizens must be prescribed by law, and the time and place within which such a restriction was in force must be clearly specified.

III. The Legislature

Legislative authority was vested in the National Assembly, consisting of the House of Representatives and the Senate. The House of Representatives would comprise

119

100 to 200 representatives, elected on an individual basis for four years by universal suffrage and secret ballot. Candidates must be at least 25, and have held Vietnamese citizenship for at least five years. The Senate would consist of 30 to 60 members, elected by list voting for six years. Half of the Senate would be elected every three years; members of the first Senate would be divided into two groups by drawing lots, one group serving six and the other three years. Candidates for the Senate must be at least 30 years of age.

Representatives and Senators would enjoy customary parliamentary immunities. They might not hold any other official position except teaching posts, and they and their spouses might not participate in bids or sign contracts with Government agencies. In cases of treason or other serious crimes, they might be removed from office by a resolution proposed by two-thirds and approved by three-quarters of the total number of members of the House concerned.

The National Assembly would vote legislation; ratify treaties and international agreements; determine declarations of war or of a state of war and the holding of peace talks; control the Government in the carrying out of national policy; and decide on the validity of the election of Representatives or Senators. Each House, with the agreement of one-third of its members, might request the Prime Minister or Government officials to appear before it to answer questions on the execution of national policy. Committee chairmen in each House might request Government officials to participate in the sessions of their committee to report on problems relating to the Ministry concerned. The Senate might open investigations into the execution of national policy and request Government agencies to produce the necessary documents.

The National Assembly could recommend the replacement of part or all of the Government by a two-thirds majority vote of the total number of Representatives and Senators. This recommendation was binding unless the President had special reasons for rejecting it. In the event of rejection, the National Assembly could override this by a three-quarters majority vote of the total number of Representatives and Senators, its recommendation being binding from the day it was voted.

Representatives, Senators and the President might submit Bills to the House of Representatives. Whether the House approved or rejected a Bill, it must transmit the Bill to the Senate within three days of its decision. If the Senate agreed with the House's viewpoint, the Bill would be transmitted to the President for promulgation or would be rejected. If the Senate did not agree with the House, it must return the Bill within three days along with an explanation for its decision. The House might then vote final approval of a Bill by a two-thirds majority of its total membership; if it was unable to reach a two-thirds majority, the Senate's view-point would be considered as approved. The President must promulgate a Bill approved by the Assembly within 15 days, or within seven days if the Assembly considered it urgent; if he did not do so it would automatically become law. He had the right, however, to propose amendments within this period; in this case the Assembly would meet in joint session, and if an absolute majority voted to reject the President's amendments the Bill would become law.

IV. The Executive

Executive authority was vested in the President. The President and Vice-President would run on a single list, would be elected by universal suffrage for four years, and might be re-elected once. They must be Vietnamese citizens by birth and 35 years of

120

age, and must have resided continuously in Vietnam for at least 10 years before the election, time spent abroad on official assignments or in political exile being considered as residence in Vietnam.

If the President's duties terminated more than a year before the end of his term of office because of death, resignation, impeachment or serious and prolonged illness, the Vice-President would assume the Presidency for three months in order to organize the election of a new President and Vice-President for a new term of office. If the President's duties terminated within a year of the end of his term, the Vice-President would assume the Presidency for the remainder of the term, except in cases of the impeachment of the President. If for any reason the Vice-President was unable to assume the Presidency, the President of the Senate would assume the office for three months in order to organize the election of a new President and Vice-President.

The President would appoint the Prime Minister and, on the latter's proposal, the members of the Government; he might reorganize all or part of the Government on his own initiative or upon the recommendation of the National Assembly. He would appoint chiefs of diplomatic missions and rectors of universities, with the Senate's approval; represent the nation in relations with foreign countries and receive the credentials of diplomatic envoys; sign international treaties and promulgate them after ratification by the Assembly; be C.-in-C. of the armed forces; bestow decorations; and exercise the right of pardon. He would determine national policy, preside over the Council of Ministers and inform each regular session of the Assembly on the state of the nation and the Government's policies. In special circumstances he might declare by decree a state of alert, curfew or emergency over all or part of the national territory; the Assembly must convene within 12 days to ratify, amend or reject such a decree. In a state of war, and when elections could not be held, the President, with the approval of two-thirds of the total membership of the Assembly, might extend the terms of office of elected bodies and appoint province chiefs.

The Vice-President would be chairman of the Culture and Education Council, the Economic and Social Council and the Ethnic Minority Council. He might not hold any other Government post.

The Prime Minister would direct the Government and the administrative agencies of the nation and would be responsible before the President for carrying out national policy. He and other Government officials might participate in sessions of the Assembly or its committees to explain matters relating to national policy.

The President, Vice-President, Prime Minister and members of the Government might not hold any position in the private sector, with or without remuneration, and their spouses might not participate in Government bids or contracts.

The President would be chairman of the National Security Council, which would study all matters relating to national defence, propose measures for the maintenance of national security and propose the declaration of states of alert, curfew, emergency or war, declarations of war and the holding of peace talks.

Province chiefs, mayors and the members of village, province and municipal councils would be elected by universal suffrage, whilst village chiefs would be elected by village councils from among their members. The Government would appoint two officials with the responsibility to assist mayors, province chiefs and village chiefs in administrative and security matters, as well as other administrative personnel. Members and heads of local government bodies might be dismissed by the President if they violated the Constitution, the law or national policy.

121

V. The Judiciary

Judges might be relieved of their functions only in cases of mental and physical incapacity, conviction or violation of discipline.

The Supreme Court would consist of nine to 15 judges or lawyers who had served at least 10 years in the judiciary, and would be chosen by the National Assembly and appointed by the President from a list elected by the Association of Judges, the Association of Prosecutors, and the Association of Lawyers. The court would interpret the Constitution. It would decide on the constitutionality of all laws and decree-laws; the constitutionality and legality of decrees and administrative decisions; the dissolution of a political party whose policy and activities opposed the republican form of government; and on appeals from lower courts. Decisions declaring a law unconstitutional or ordering the dissolution of a political party would require a three-fourths vote of the total number of Supreme Court justices.

The Judicial Council, which would be elected by the judges from among their own number, would propose the appointment, promotion, transfer and disciplining of judges, and would advise the Supreme Court in matters relating to the judiciary.

VI. Special Institutions

A Special Court, consisting of the President of the Supreme Court as chairman, five Representatives and five Senators, could remove from office the President, Vice-President, Prime Minister, Ministers, Secretaries of State, Supreme Court justices and members of the Inspectorate in cases of treason or other high crimes. A motion to bring charges and citing reasons therefore must be signed by more than one-half of the total number of Representatives and Senators, and approved by a two-thirds majority vote of their total number. In the case of the President or Vice-President, the motion must be signed by two-thirds of the total number and approved by three-fourths. The functions of the accused would be suspended from the date of the decision to bring charges until the Special Court's decision was rendered. The Special Court would decide removal from office by a three-fourths vote of its membership, and in the case of the President and Vice-President by a four-fifths vote. After being removed from office the accused might be tried by an ordinary court.

The Inspectorate would include from nine to 18 inspectors, one-third designated by the National Assembly, one-third by the President and one-third by the Supreme Court, and would be empowered to investigate personnel of all public and private agencies on suspicion of being directly or indirectly engaged in corruption, speculation, influence-peddling or acts harmful to the national interest; to inspect accounts of public agencies and corporations; and to audit the property of personnel of public agencies, including the President, the Vice-President, the Prime Minister, National Assembly members and the President of the Supreme Court. In the case of the chairman and members of the Inspectorate, the audit of personal property would be conducted by the Supreme Court. The Inspectorate would announce publicly the results of its investigations, and would propose disciplinary measures against guilty persons or request prosecution by competent courts.

The Armed Forces Council would advise the President on matters relating to the armed forces, especially promotion, transfer and disciplining of military personnel of all ranks.

The Culture and Education Council, one-third of whose members would be appointed by the President and two-thirds designated by public and private cultural and educational organizations and by parent-teacher associations, would advise the Government on cultural and educational policy; brief the National Assembly on related matters; and contribute ideas before the Assembly debated laws relating to culture and education.

The Economic and Social Council, one-third of whose members would be appointed by the President and two-thirds by industrial and trade organizations, trade unions and economic and social associations, would similarly advise the Government and the Assembly on economic and social matters.

The Ethnic Council, one-third of whose members would be appointed by the President and two-thirds designated by the ethnic minorities, would advise the Government and the Assembly on matters affecting the minorities.

VII. Political Parties and Opposition

Political parties, including opposition parties, might be organized and operate freely, according to the procedures and conditions prescribed by law. Progress towards a two-party system would be encouraged.

VIII. Amending the Constitution

The President or an absolute majority of the total number of Representatives or Senators might propose amendments to the Constitution. A joint committee would study the proposed amendment and report to joint plenary sessions of the Assembly. A resolution to amend the Constitution must be approved by two-thirds of the total number of Representatives and Senators.

IX. Transitional Provisions

The Constitution took effect from the date it was promulgated, and the Provisional Charter of June 19, 1965, was then automatically invalidated.

During the transitional period the Constituent Assembly would draft laws for the election of the President and Vice-President, the Senate and the House of Representatives; establish a list of candidates; announce the result of the presidential election; draft laws organizing the Supreme Court and the Inspectorate, and political party and press regulations; and ratify treaties. From the time the first President took office the Constituent Assembly would assume legislative powers until the first National Assembly was convened. The Directory and Cabinet would continue in office until the first President took office. The courts would continue to exercise judicial authority until the judicial organs prescribed in the Constitution were established. During the first presidential term the President would appoint province chiefs.

The election of the President and Vice-President would take place not later than six months after the promulgation of the Constitution; the election of the National Assembly and the organization of the Supreme Court and Inspectorate not later than 12 months after the date the President assumed office; and the establishment of the other structures prescribed by the Constitution not later than two years after the establishment of the National Assembly.

Presidential Election

The Presidential Candidates

The Provisional National Assembly (the name assumed by the Constituent Assembly after the promulgation of the Constitution) decided on May 16 that the President should be elected by a plurality of votes, and rejected a proposal that if no candidate received more than 30 per cent of the votes a second ballot should be held to enable the electorate to choose between the two leading candidates. By June 30, the final date for the reception of nominations, 18 candidates had been put forward.

A group of senior generals held a series of meetings from June 28-30 to consider the situation created by the opposing candidatures of General Nguyen Van Thieu, Marshal Nguyen Cao Ky, and General Duong Van Minh, which threatened to split the armed forces. During long and heated discussions, General Thieu was reported to have accused Marshal Ky of using the Government machinery to advance his candidature by unfair means. It was finally decided on June 30 that General Thieu and Marshal Ky should run on a single list, with the former as the presidential and the latter as the vice-presidential candidate—a decision which was regarded as a serious setback to Marshal Ky's political ambitions. It was also officially announced that "for reasons of national security" General Minh and other exiled generals would not be allowed to return to Vietnam for the time being.

The Assembly approved 17 of the 18 tickets on July 1, including that of General Minh and his fellow-candidate, Tran Ngoc Lieng, who had resigned from Marshal Ky's Government in November 1966 as a protest against its "police State" methods. The only ticket rejected was that of Tran Thuong Nhon and Nguyen Van Hung, two little-known figures whose documents were held to be not in order. The candidatures were then referred to a central electoral council, headed by a judge of the Court of Appeals, for consideration.

The election committee of the Assembly, however, decided on July 17, by eight votes to four, to recommend that General Thieu and Marshal Ky should not be allowed to contest the elections, on the ground that by continuing to act as Chief of State and Prime Minister they had violated the legal requirement that civil servants must take unpaid leave before seeking office. The military leaders thereupon called an emergency meeting, and the police and some military units were put on the alert.

The Assembly's final debate on the candidatures took place during the night of July 18-19 in an atmosphere of tension, watched from the gallery by General Nguyen Ngoc Loan, who was accompanied by two armed bodyguards; some deputies afterwards stated that they had feared that the Assembly would be dissolved if it rejected General Thieu's candidature. During the debate some deputies maintained that the term "civil servants" clearly did not apply to the Chief of State and the Prime Minister, whilst others expressed the fear that if they remained in office they would take advantage of their positions to ensure their election. It was finally decided to accept their candidature by 56 votes to 19.

The Assembly rejected General Minh's candidature on the ground that Tran Ngoc Lieng had formerly held French citizenship, and that of Au Truong Tranh because of his alleged neutralist sympathies, despite the protest of a member who asked why Marshal Ky had kept an alleged pro-Communist in his Government. Five minor candidates were also eliminated for various reasons, including Tran Thuong Nhon, whose candidature had been granted reconsideration

As a result of the Assembly's decision, 11 presidential and 11 vice-presidential candidates remained in the election.

Marshal Ky announced on July 19 that the press censorship would be lifted until the elections; the censorship had previously been criticized by Phan Khac Suu in a letter to the Directory, as well as by Au Truong Thanh, and the U.S. Ambassador, Mr. Ellsworth Bunker, was reported to have made representations to the Government on the subject. The laws forbidding Communist or "neutralist" propaganda remained in force, however; a Saigon newspaper was suspended on this pretext on Aug. 14 and two others on Sept. 2, including the militant Buddhists' organ *Than Chung*, which had the largest circulation in the country.

The Election Campaign

The election campaign officially opened on Aug. 3, a month before polling day. Seven of the candidates, including Phan Khac Suu and Tran Van Huong, announced on Aug. 10 that as they had received no reply from the Government to their request for better facilities, they would suspend their campaign until they received an assurance that there would be "an end to harassment". They reversed their decision on Aug. 12, however, and began their campaign four days later.

125

The civilian candidates made repeated allegations that their supporters were being intimidated by the police; these allegations were described as "ridiculous" by General Thieu and Marshal Ky on Aug. 19. However, they announced that an inquiry had been ordered, and that if it were proved that any officials had used illegal pressure to obtain votes for them they would be punished.

Colonel Pham Van Lieu (a former chief of police) and two other officers were arrested on Sept. 1 on charges of taking part in Phan Khac Suu's election campaign. *Le Monde* reported that 95 per cent of the election posters, all of which were printed by the Government, bore the portraits of the military candidates.

During the election campaign the question of peace negotiations emerged as the main issue.

General Nguyen Van Thieu declared on Aug. 3 that the way to end the war was to convince the Communists that they could in no way inflict a defeat, either militarily or politically, on South Vietnam. As the campaign proceeded, however, he laid increasing emphasis on peace negotiations. He told a press conference on Aug. 8 that if elected he would invite the North Vietnamese to take part in peace talks, and that if he were convinced that a temporary halt to the bombing would help towards this end he would ask the United States to stop it ; he did not believe that talks with the National Liberation Front would result in peace, however, because it was "merely a tool of North Vietnam's aggression". Talks with Hanoi would be on the basis, not of the Geneva Agreements, but of "the reality of Vietnam's partition".

The most outspoken advocate of peace was Truong Dinh Dzu, who chose a white dove as his election symbol. He put forward the following policy: (1) Immediate and unconditional ending of the bombing of North Vietnam and of the Viet Cong zones, and of North Vietnamese infiltration and military activity in South Vietnam. (2) Negotiations with the North Vietnamese Government and the National Liberation Front. (3) A new Geneva Conference, with Asian countries taking part, in order to obtain firm guarantees for an honourable peace; these guarantees might be provided either by the progressive replacement of the U.S. troops by a U.N. force or even by the extension of the U.S. presence in Vietnam. He rejected the theory that the National Liberation Front was a "tool" of the North Vietnamese Government; thought that only about 30 per cent of its members were Communists, and that most of them were sincere nationalists; and pointed out that with 130,000 men in arms it represented a political force to be reckoned with.

General Thieu Elected President

Voting in the presidential election took place on Sept. 3. The Viet Cong carried out a number of acts of terrorism during the voting, in which 49 civilians were officially stated to have been killed and 204 wounded.

126

Only three polling stations out of 8,824 were prevented from functioning, however, all of them in Quangtri province. *Le Monde* commented that "the guerrillas have considerably increased the number of terrorist acts during the pre-electoral period, without seriously trying to disturb the elections, to which they do not attach much importance".

The official election results, announced on Sept. 5, showed that 4,868,281 people, or 83 per cent of the 5,853,384 electors, had voted, and that 4,735,404 valid votes had been cast. The largest number of votes, 1,649,561 or 34.8 per cent, was obtained by General Thieu.

He was believed to have gained most of his support from the Army, the Civil Service and minority groups such as the Roman Catholic refugees from North Vietnam, the Montagnards and the Cambodian and Chinese communities. He failed to win first place in any of the major cities, but gained heavily in the Mekong delta and in the Central Highlands.

A striking feature of the election was the strong support (17 per cent of the total vote) given to the "peace" candidate, **Truong Dinh Dzu,** who obtained 817,120 votes, headed the poll in four western provinces (Kien Phong, Tay Ninh, Hau Nghia, and Binh Duong) and took second place in five other provinces, in all of which heavy fighting had recently taken place. *The Guardian* commented : "That such a largely unknown candidate should gain second place in the election indicates the strength of the feeling in South Vietnam for ending the war", whilst *The Daily Telegraph* .observed that "Dzu's early campaign references to peace and talks with the Communists' National Liberation Front attracted attention. The choice of a white dove as his election symbol is thought to have had special meaning to war-weary peasants."

Phan Khac Suu, who was thought to have benefited from the support of the militant Buddhists, with a total of 513,374 votes, took first place in the cities of Hué and Danang and in the northern province of Thua Thien. **Tran Van Huong,** gaining 474,100 votes, won his only success in Saigon, where he defeated General Thieu by the narrow margin of 3,000 votes.

The civilian candidates alleged on Sept. 4 that the elections had been "fraudulent". Truong Dinh Dzu claimed that his supporters had been refused ballot papers at some Saigon polling stations on the pretext that supplies had run out, similar allegations being made by Phan Khac Suu and Tran Van Huong. These allegations were denied by a spokesman for Marshal Ky, who declared that "if there had been fraud we should have had a bigger majority".

Assembly Confirms Election Results

Eight of the 10 civilian candidates in the election submitted a complaint to the Assembly on Sept. 7 listing five charges of irregularities against General Thieu and Marshal Ky, who were alleged to have taken advantage of their official positions during the campaign and to have used more radio and television time than that allotted equally to all the candidates, and calling for the results to be nullified. An attempt by the civilian candidates to hold a press conference on the same day was broken up by the police.

During the night of Sept. 29-30 the election committee of the Assembly decided by 16 votes to two, with one abstention, to recommend that the presidential election should be declared invalid because of the irregularities which had occurred, and the Assembly met on Sept. 30 to decide on the question in an atmosphere of tension. The next day it decided to reject all but eight of the 38 complaints of irregularities in the election. During a passionate debate on the following day some deputies accused others of having received 50,000,000 piastres in bribes from General Thieu and from "foreigners" to vote in favour of validation, these allegations being angrily denied. A few minutes before midnight, the legal deadline for their decision, the Assembly decided by 58 votes to 43, with one abstention and four spoilt ballots, to declare the election valid. Phan Khac Suu refused to announce the result, and instead announced his immediate resignation from the presidency of the Assembly, declaring, "I do not wish to bear the responsibility for this injustice before history."

.

The Senatorial Elections

The elections to the 60-member Senate, which were held on Sept. 3 at the same time as the presidential election, were contested by 48 lists each comprising 10 candidates; 16 other lists had been excluded from the ballot by the central election committee, including two put forward by the militant Buddhists. Half of the candidates issued on Aug. 24 a joint protest alleging that the Government was intervening in the election campaign.

The large number of candidates apparently caused much confusion among the electors. The voting figures suggested that many people who voted in the presidential election did not cast all their six ballots, and *The New York Times* reported that according to American correspondents "many voters, confronted with a choice of six among 48 unfamiliar Senate tickets, gave up in confusion and picked from one to six ballots at random".

128

The final results showed that 40 of the 60 seats had been won by lists which were largely composed of Catholics and of supporters of the late President Ngo Dinh Diem—the Catholics' success being attributed to their strict voting discipline and to divisions among their opponents.

The *Financial Times* subsequently commented on the new Senate: "The vagaries of the electoral system itself have produced an almost crazily unrepresentative body of 60 Senators. Almost half of them are Roman Catholics, and a good third are northerners, that is, exiles who abandoned North Vietnam after the 1954 Geneva Agreement. There is also a fair sprinkling of people associated with the last years of President Diem's rule. By contrast, there will be no spokesmen for the more militant wing of the Buddhist Church in the Senate nor, equally important, were any politicians who represent the self-consciously native southerners elected...."

A number of lists regarded as supporting Marshal Ky failed to secure election; *The New York Times* described Marshal Ky as "the big loser" in the elections, and commented that he "was reported to have counted heavily on the election of a Senate favourable to him to aid in his continuing subterranean power struggle with General Thieu".

U.S. Observers' Report on Election – Foreign Press Comment

The elimination of a number of candidates from the presidential and senatorial elections, and the accusations against the Government by the civilian candidates during the election campaign, aroused considerable uneasiness in the United States, especially among sections of the Democratic Party. A statement issued on Aug. 10 by 57 Democratic members of the House of Representatives urged President Johnson to "make the strongest representations that steps be taken promptly to prevent a further eroding of confidence in the elections", and continued: "If the Government authorities of South Vietnam continue to refuse to assure free and fair elections, they should be informed that the United States may very well undertake a serious reappraisal of its policies in Vietnam."

During a debate in the U.S. Senate on the following day 12 leading members of both parties strongly criticized the conduct of the election

129

campaign in South Vietnam. In reply to this criticism, the South Vietnamese Ambassador, Bui Diem, invited Congress to send observers to South Vietnam to ensure that the elections were free and "open to scrutiny by all". Senator Mansfield (the Democratic leader in the Senate), however, commented that he could see "no reason why Congress should involve itself in this matter", whilst the Republican leader, Senator Dirksen, observed that, "if we did anything of that kind, the losers in the election would be certain to blame Congress for their defeat and to contend that the election had been rigged".

President Johnson announced on Aug. 23 that 20 prominent Americans had accepted an invitation to visit South Vietnam and report on the fairness of the election campaign and the voting. The party included Senators Edmund Muskie (Dem.), Bourke Hickenlooper (Rep.), and George Murphy (Rep.); several others who had been invited, including Senator Fulbright (chairman of the Senate Foreign Relations Committee), declined the invitation. The observers, who left Washington on Aug. 28 and returned on Sept. 6, reported on their return that the elections had been as free and fair as circumstances permitted.

Some foreign commentators, however, expressed a certain scepticism, pointing out that the U.S. observers had spent only a few days in the country, that the itinerary had been arranged by the American Embassy and the South Vietnamese Government, and that none of them spoke Vietnamese and hence could not converse with ordinary people.

Le Monde commented on the voting results: "The most striking fact of this election without surprises is the defeat of the generals in the large towns. It is true that voting conditions there are very different from those in the countryside, and that because of the presence of journalists and observers the civilian opposition there doubtless had more opportunity to express itself. . . . Paradoxically, it is the zones where the Liberation Front is strongest which supply the figures most favourable to the Government, notably the High Plateaux and the delta region. The Chief of State also heads the list in Central Vietnam, which is known to be the stronghold of the Buddhist opposition. . . . The conditions in which the elections took place leave the majority of observers sceptical. . . ."

Inauguration of Senate
The Senate was officially inaugurated by President Thieu on Oct. 11.

In his speech on this occasion President Thieu said that "we will always welcome all peace initiatives, provided those initiatives contribute to bring a just and lasting

130

peace, but if the enemy continues his aggression, we shall intensify our military and political efforts". He called on Opposition elements to show a constructive and responsible attitude, and promised to "respect the rights of the Opposition as a political reality of democracy".

Elections to House of Representatives

The elections to the House of Representatives took place on Oct. 22 the 137 seats being contested by 1,140 candidates. 72.9 per cent of the electorate voted, although in Saigon the figure was only 57.8 per cent; the reduced poll, as compared with the presidential and senatorial elections, was attributed in part to the large number of candidates, which made it difficult for voters to decide whom to support. The number of terrorist incidents was lower than during the presidential election; 22 people were killed, including 11 of the Viet Cong, and 29 wounded.

As the candidates contested the elections as individuals rather than as party representatives, estimates of the strengths of the various groups in the new House differed widely.

The Daily Telegraph's estimate, based on incomplete returns, was as follows: the Democratic Alliance (pro-Government), the militant Buddhists and the Movement for the Restoration of the South (which was opposed to the strong military and North Vietnamese element in the Government), about 20 each; Roman Catholics and the Farmers', Workers' and Soldiers' list, 10 to 20 each; the Hoa Hao, the Caodaists, the Dai Viet Party and the Kuominatang, five to 10 each; the Struggle for Democracy Front, one; Independents, 30 to 40. *Le Monde,* on the other hand, estimated that the Catholics and the North Vietnamese refugees had each won about a quarter of the seats, and the Buddhists 46, whilst the *Neue Zürcher Zeitung* gave the number of Catholics as 20 to 30.

Inauguration of President Nguyen Van Thieu

President Thieu took the oath of office on Oct. 31, in the presence of Vice-President Humphrey of the United States, officials and journalists. Strict security precautions were taken to keep the general public away from the ceremony, as it was feared that the militant Buddhists would take advantage of it to stage hostile demonstrations.

In his inaugural speech President Thieu said: "I confirm once more my direct offer to the North Vietnamese Government to sit down at the conference table, so that the Governments of the North and the South can seek and find together ways of ending the war." Members of the National Liberation Front were offered a choice: "Those who believe in Marxism must return to North Vietnam, the others must join us and work with us". He claimed that during the past two years 149,000 of the enemy had been killed, 23,000 had been captured, and 55,000 had surrendered; that 1,978 hamlets with a population of 3,498,000 had been "pacified"; and that 750 miles of roads had been reopened. President Thieu summed up the main points of his policy as follows: (1) The morale and living conditions of the armed forces must be improved. (2) The population of the towns must accept greater sacrifices, and the well-to-do must "restrain their life of luxury" in order to eliminate the "shocking contrasts" between the countryside and the towns. (3) It was necessary to build democracy and reform society, to establish constitutional institutions as soon as possible and to institute social justice.

About 1,000 political prisoners were released under an amnesty granted in connexion with the installation of General Thieu as President; they included militant Buddhists and members of the Viet Cong. In addition, it was reported on Nov. 2 that 4,320 South Vietnamese detained as Viet Cong suspects during military operations would also be released.

Cabinet Formed by Nguyen Van Loc

President Thieu accepted the Cabinet's resignation on Oct. 31, and asked Nguyen Van Loc to form a Government. The new Cabinet, the membership of which was announced on Nov. 9, consisted of 17 Ministers, two Secretaries of State, and seven Under-Secretaries.

"Struggle for Democracy Front"

Truong Dinh Dzu, Phan Khac Suu, Vu Hong Khanh and four of the other presidential candidates announced on Sept. 14 that they had formed a "Struggle for Democracy Front", together with candidates defeated in the senatorial elections. The movement was supported by students of Saigon University, who staged a sit-in strike on Sept. 13 and issued a statement denouncing the elections as "conducive to another Diem-like dictatorship", and by the militant Buddhists; the Buddhist leader Thich Tri Quang appeared at a press conference together with Truong Dinh Dzu on Sept. 24. From Saigon the agitation spread to the Buddhist strongholds of Danang, where a state of emergency was declared on Sept. 15, and Hué; demonstrations by students and monks took place in all three cities on Sept. 24. At the same time sections of the Vietnamese Press launched a violent anti-American campaign, accusing Washington of interfering in South Vietnam's internal affairs; a Government communiqué (Sept. 14) commented that since the suspension of the censorship some newspapers had shown "a certain regrettable negligence", and that the Government might be forced to take "appropriate measures against foreign press agencies spreading false news".

X. THE AFTERMATH OF THE TET OFFENSIVE OF 1968

During the Tet (lunar new year) holiday the Viet Cong launched a general offensive on Jan. 30-Feb. 1, 1968, Saigon, Hué and many other towns, as well as military installations, being attached. They were expelled from all the towns which they had penetrated by Feb. 24, but only after heavy fighting which reduced large areas of many of the towns to ruins and caused numerous casualties among the civilian population, whilst the withdrawal of U.S. and South Vietnamese troops to protect the towns enabled the Viet Cong to regain control of much of the countryside.

Reorganization of Military Command and Provincial Administration

Following the Tet offensive, President Thieu carried out a major reorganization of the military command and the provincial administration in February and March 1968. The commanders of the 2nd Corps (the central highlands and central coastal provinces) and the 4th Corps (the Mekong delta) were replaced on Feb. 23. The President signed a decree on March 1, 1968, transferring responsibility for the appointment of province chiefs from the four corps commanders to himself, seven province chiefs being dismissed for alleged corruption and incompetence on March 11 and four more on March 26.

Temporary Detention of Opposition Leaders

It was announced on Feb. 21, 1968, that four prominent political figures had been placed in "protective custody". These were Thich Tri Quang, the militant Buddhist leader; Truong Dinh Dzu, who had taken second place in the 1967 presidential election on a peace platform; Au Truong Thanh, a former Economics Minister who had been disqualified from standing in the election because of his alleged neutralist views; and Ho Thong Minh, a former Minister in Ngo Dinh Diem's Government before the latter's assumption of the Presidency, who had lived in Paris since 1955 and had returned to Saigon for a short visit. A large number of other persons regarded as opponents of the regime, several of whom had advocated ending the war through negotiations with the N.L.F., were arrested during the next few days, including Vu Hong Khanh (another candidate in the presidential election), Tran Huu Quyen (general secretary of the Vietnamese Confederation of Labour), other trade union leaders, Buddhist monks, doctors, lawyers, professors and students.

Ho Thong Minh, who with Truong Dinh Dzu and Au Truong Thanh had gone on hunger strike, was released on April 11 and ordered to leave for France immediately. Truong Dinh Dzu and Au Truong Thanh were freed two days later, and Thich Tri Quang on June 30, 1968.

Trials of Truong Dinh Dzu

Truong Dinh Dzu was tried on various charges between September 1967 and May 1968.

Truong Dinh Dzu was first charged on Sept. 11 with having embezzled money in 1957, issued a bad cheque in 1962 and illegally transferred $11,500 to an American bank in 1966.

He strongly denied all three charges, which he maintained had been brought for political reasons. He was sentenced *in absentia* on Sept. 15 to a total of nine months' imprisonment and a fine of 3,270,000 piastres (£14,600) on the second and third charges, but was acquitted of the embezzlement charge.

Truong Dinh Dzu alleged after his conviction that it showed that "justice is not independent in Vietnam and the judges receive their orders from the Government", and was subsequently charged with contempt of court. He was arrested on Sept. 29 together with Vu Hong Khanh, who was released shortly after; Truong Dinh Dzu himself went on hunger strike in prison, and was released in consequence on Oct. 5. His sentence was confirmed on Oct. 20, but he gave notice that he would appeal against it.

He was rearrested on May 1, 1968, and charged with conduct "detrimental to the anti-Communist spirit of the people and the armed forces" as he had given an interview on April 14 to the Saigon correspondent of *The Times* in which, commenting on President Thieu's policy of regarding the N.L.F. as North Vietnamese "puppets", he said: "On that basis no contact with the N.L.F. is possible, and it is impossible to get real peace in South Vietnam. It is necessary to talk with the N.L.F. and discuss the conditions of a political settlement with them. Without that it is impossible to get a cease-fire. We should let them operate as a political party in the South." Many reasonable people, he continued, realized that "we must be prepared to talk with the N.L.F., but the Government always claims that it will arrest or destroy people who propose talks with the N.L.F.". On the possibility of a coalition Government he said: "There are many non-Communist elements in the N.L.F., and those people can enter a Cabinet and a coalition Government. I think the N.L.F. are realistic, and know it is not the time for the Communists to take over this country."

In an interview with the United Press International Truong Dinh Dzu said on April 16 that it was impossible to win the war unless the Government's forces were 10 times stronger than those of the N.L.F. It would ultimately be necessary to come to terms with the Front, but such an agreement was impossible so long as the present regime remained in power in Saigon.

After his rearrest, he was tried by a military court on the above charge on July 26. For the defence, his counsel contended that the trial violated the freedom of speech guaranteed by the Constitution, and that Truong Dinh Dzu's statements were compatible with President Thieu's policy that non-Communist members of the N.L.F. could be reintegrated into the country's political life if they laid down their arms.

He was, however, convicted and sentenced to five years' hard labour and confiscation of his property.

A Government spokesman announced on May 28, 1969, that Truong Dinh Dzu would be moved from the prison island of Poulo Condor to Saigon for medical treatment. His son, David Truong, alleged at a press conference in New York on June 28 that the Government were letting his father "die of hunger in prison in order to eliminate him from the political scene".

Trial and Imprisonment of Thich Thien Minh —
Abolition of Special Military Tribunal

In his first public statement since his release from "protective custody" [see page 134], Thich Tri Quang appealed on Nov. 18, 1968, for a cease-fire as a first step towards a political settlement in Vietnam, and during the next three months the militant Buddhists organized a campaign of demonstrations in favour of peace which attracted growing support. After Thich Tinh Khiet, the head of the United Buddhist Church, had issued an appeal for Buddhists to make sacrifices in the cause of peace, a monk burned himself alive in a village near Saigon on Feb. 12, 1969, this being the 28th fire suicide in South Vietnam since 1963.

The Ministry of Information announced on Feb. 4, 1969, that persons found in possession of "subversive material", including newspapers, gramophone records and photographs, would be tried by a military court. Thich Thien Minh, the head of the Buddhist youth movement, whose sermons were considered "defamatory" by the Government, was given an official warning on the same day. President Thieu declared in a speech on Feb. 5 that the Government would "crush" Buddhist monks and Catholic priests who demanded "a pro-Communist peace", and stated that he had ordered province chiefs to arrest them if necessary.

Thich Thien Minh was arrested on Feb. 23, together with about 40 Buddhist students, and was sentenced to 10 years' hard labour by the special military tribunal on March 15 for "harbouring traitors" and illegal possession of weapons and documents. The court also sentenced eight youths tried with him to terms ranging from three to 20 years, and ordered the confiscation of the Buddhist youth headquarters. Thich Thien Minh was convicted by another military court on March 17 of harbouring deserters, and was sentenced to five years' imprisonment, to run concurrently with his previous sentence.

Protests against the sentences on Thich Thien Minh were issued on March 21 by the National Salvation Front [see page 144] and on April 9 by 40 members of the House of Representatives. President Thieu granted an amnesty on May 25 under which Thich Thien Minh's sentence was reduced to three years' imprisonment, and on the following day abolished the special military tribunal, the abolition of which had been demanded by the National Assembly on March 8. This measure annulled the first sentence passed on Thich Thien Minh, and made it necessary for his case to be re-tried by a civil court.

However, on Oct. 29 President Thieu announced an amnesty for 310 prisoners, Thich Thien Minh being one of 64 who were released from prison.

Government Measures against Corruption
General Thieu had stated on Aug. 25, 1968, that 50 officers, ranging from generals to second lieutenants, would shortly appear before the

Armed Services' Disciplinary Council on charges of corruption and incompetence. This announcement was regarded as a reply to accusations of corruption in the armed forces, especially among officers assigned to civilian duties since Marshal Ky's Government took power, which had been made by the civilian candidates in the presidential election. An official accused of having embezzled over 2,500,000 piastres had previously been sentenced to death on April 1, 1968.

American criticisms of the prevalence of corruption in South Vietnam became increasingly outspoken in the early months of 1968, as a result of the scandal caused by the wholesale theft of relief supplies intended for the victims of the Tet offensive. *Le Monde* reported on March 16 that the greater part of the supplies sent to Hué by the Government and the Americans had not reached the 17,000 refugees; that according to U.S. sources food had been distributed to them only three times in two weeks, instead of daily as had been planned; and that only the families of soldiers and the police had received the rations intended for them.

A report published on March 6, 1968, by 22 U.S. advisers who had been working in economic aid organizations for four years declared that "corruption in Vietnam forms part of everyday life and has spread to all levels of the Government and society", and expressed doubt whether "there is any possibility of achieving a certain degree of honesty and integrity in Vietnamese official circles". A sub-committee of the U.S. Senate headed by Senator Edward Kennedy reported on June 23, 1968, that "rampant and inconceivable corruption" was frustrating U.S. efforts to help the 4,000,000 displaced persons in South Vietnam, and was depriving the country of more than half the medical supplies sent by the United States. The report estimated that about three-quarters of the $43 resettlement allowance given to each refugee was being diverted by corrupt officials.

In a broadcast on March 21, 1968, President Thieu gave warning that the penalties for bribery, corruption and embezzlement among military officers and civil servants would be strictly enforced, and that in the worst cases the death penalty would be carried out. Tran Van Huong announced on June 29 that in order to "restore the people's confidence in the Government" he would dismiss 50 to 100 district chiefs. [The 44 provinces are divided into about 250 districts, in each of which the administration is headed by an Army officer.] By replacing 20 to 40 per cent of the district chiefs and several province chiefs, Tran Van Huong said he hoped to set an example for lower-ranking officials, as if every corrupt official were removed "we wouldn't have enough people left to run the country and we haven't enough jails to put all the corrupt officials in".

Four officers were sentenced to death for diversion of public funds on March 15, 1968, and eight others to hard labour, and on March 26 a junior officer was condemned to death for embezzling 3,365,692 piastres ($28,050 at the official exchange rate). A colonel, a sergeant, and a civilian contractor were sentenced to life imprisonment on corruption charges on Aug. 8. Several members of the "anti-corruption youth" groups set up by Marshal Ky when Prime Minister in 1965 were themselves sentenced to terms of imprisonment for corruption in October; one of them, who was sentenced to seven years' hard labour, was convicted of selling forged military service cards at 70,000 piastres (about £250 each). It was announced on July 9, 1969, that General Nguyen Van Toan (commander of the 2nd infantry division) and Dr. Bui Hoanh (chief of Quang Ngai province) had been dismissed for organizing an illegal traffic in cinnamon; Dr. Hoanh was stated to have issued illegal permits for the transport of the cinnamon, which was carried in military lorries supplied by General Toan.

Decline of Political Influence of Vice-President Ky

The immediate effect of the Tet offensive was to increase the political influence of Vice-President Nguyen Cao Ky, whose relations with President Thieu were known to be strained. As the President was absent from Saigon when the attack began, Vice-President Ky established on Feb. 1, 1968, a "National Reconstruction Committee", which virtually assumed the functions of the Government, and a propaganda campaign was launched in favour of a revision of the Constitution which would enable him to take over the Premiership. Criticism in the Assembly of the inadequacy of the defences of the capital and the destruction caused in its reconquest forced Vice-President Ky to dissolve the committee on Feb. 20, however, and the political developments of the next four months further weakened his position.

President Thieu's purge of province chiefs in March 1968 enabled him to replace officials appointed during Marshal Ky's Premiership by his own supporters. Nguyen Van Loc, a friend and political associate of Vice-President Ky, was replaced in May by Tran Van Huong, whose hostility to the Vice-President was well-known. Vice-President Ky still retained powerful supporters in military circles, including Brigadier-General Nguyen Ngoc Loan (the chief of the national police, who controlled a force of 72,000 men), Lieut.-General Le Nguyen Khang (commander of the 3rd Corps and military governor of Saigon), Colonel Van Van Cua (the Mayor of Saigon) and General Nguyen Duc Thang. General Loan was seriously wounded on May 5, however; Colonel Cua was also wounded on June 2 by a rocket fired from a U.S. helicopter; and General Khang resigned on June 5 because of this incident, all three being replaced by supporters of President Thieu. These in turn carried out a purge of their predecessors' appointments; Colonel Tran Van Hai, the new chief of police, dismissed eight of the police commissioners of Saigon on June 15, 1968.

Following these changes, Vice-President Ky retired to the coastal town of Nha Trang, and on June 12, 1968, resigned the post of chairman of the People's Self-Defence Committee (a body responsible for the military training of the civilian

138

population), to which he had been appointed on May 3. Several generals also showed their dissatisfaction; General Nguyen Van Vy (the Defence Minister), General Cao Van Vien (the Chief of Staff), and General Khang boycotted the ceremony on June 16 at which Major-General Nguyen Van Minh assumed command of the 3rd Corps, and General Thang resigned on the same day. This demonstration led to wide-spread rumours that the Vice-President was planning a military coup, and tanks and additional troops were posted around the Presidential Palace. Vice-President Ky flew back to Saigon on June 17, however, and denied in a broadcast that he had any such intention. General Nguyen Viet Thanh succeeded General Thang as commander of the 4th Corps on July 1.

The General Mobilization Law

The Senate had previously adopted on Dec. 20, 1967, with only one dissentient, a resolution calling on President Thieu to suspend his decree of Oct. 24 lowering the conscription age from 20 to 18; this vote was regarded an an anti-American gesture, as the decree was widely believed in Saigon to have been issued under pressure from the U.S. military authorities. A request by President Thieu that in order to control inflation and suppress corruption he should be given emergency powers for one year to issue decrees on economic and other matters without the National Assembly's consent was rejected by the House of Representatives on March 1, 1968, by 85 votes to 10, and by the Senate on March 7 by 40 votes to three.

President Thieu submitted to the Assembly on April 10, 1968, a two-line Bill providing for general mobilization of the country's manpower and resources and for the raising of the maximum age for military service from 33 to 45, and asked that it should be passed quickly. The defence committee of the House of Representatives, however, rejected the Bill as too vague and drafted its own, which was passed on May 10; this limited conscription into the regular forces to men between 18 and 38, and provided for compulsory service in the civilian Self-Defence Corps for men between 16 and 18 and between 39 and 45 and for exemption of key workers. Although the Senate approved the President's Bill with minor amendments, the House rejected the Senate's version on May 28 and reaffirmed its own.

At a joint session of the two Houses on June 14-15 agreement was reached on a compromise measure, which was signed by President Thieu on June 19. This provided for an increase in the size of the armed forces from 775,000 to 910,000 by the end of 1968; authorized the Government to conscript all men between 18 and 38 into the regular forces, and those over 16 and between 39 and 50 into the Self-Defence Corps; and laid down that if necessary, youths of 17 and men between 39 and 43 might be conscripted for non-combatant service in the regular forces.

Cabinet Formed by Tran Van Huong

The Prime Minister, Nguyen Van Loc, whose Government had been strongly criticized in the National Assembly for its failure to win popular support and its ineffective conduct of the war, tendered his resignation on May 18, 1968, whereupon President Nguyen Van Thieu asked Tran Van Huong to form a Cabinet.

In his first broadcast as Prime Minister, on May 28, Tran Van Huong said that his Government's immediate objectives were (1) to restore the authority of the State and ensure the implementation of the Constitution; (2) to step up the campaign against corruption; (3) to improve living standards, priority being given to the rehabilitation of refugees and war victims; and (4) to take the initiative in the search for peace.

On the question of peace, Tran Van Huong said that the Government was taking the initiative by seeking to play a key role at the conference table in eventual negotiations, and by advocating direct negotiations between Saigon and Hanoi, so as to allow the Vietnamese people to solve their own problems themselves. He appealed to all Vietnamese of goodwill on the other side to end the "fratricidal way", and to "join in the search for a satisfactory solution for our fatherland in all serenity". If the other side expected to obtain a military victory by the "shelling, arson and slaughter of honest and harmless citizens", however, the Government was "determined to resist to the bitter end". On the other points in his programme he said that the war had caused the law to be despised by the powerful, and he was determined to have the Constitution respected and the law applied to all. Leading officials must set the example in honesty, and rewards and punishments must be fairly applied to all.

Establishment of Administrative Council, National Planning Council and Supreme Court

President Thieu had announced on March 21, 1968, that an Administrative Council would be established to review the responsibilities, organization and functioning of the Civil Service, and a National Planning Council to outline the broad objectives of the Government's economic policy and of the major development projects financed by the national budget or assisted by international organizations. The two bodies held their first meetings on June 5 and 6, 1968, respectively.

Each council consisted of the President as chairman and five permanent members; in addition, the Director-General of the Civil Service and a number of other high officials were *ex-officio* members of the Administrative Council, and experts on administrative and economic questions might be invited to attend the sessions of the two councils. Nguyen Dinh Xuong (Special Commissioner for Administrative Reform) became secretary-general of the Administrative Council, and Ton That Trinh (Commissioner-General for National Plans) secretary-general of the National Planning Council.

A Bill establishing the Supreme Court was passed by the National Assembly on Aug. 30, 1968, and signed by President Thieu on Sept. 4. The nine judges were chosen by a plenary session of the Assembly on Oct. 15 for a six-year term from a list of 30 drawn up by legal bodies, and took the oath of office on Oct. 22.

State of Alert in Saigon

President Thieu issued a decree late in the evening of Oct. 8. 1968, putting the armed forces on the alert, and anti-aircraft guns were placed on the roof of the Presidential Palace, no official explanation being given of the reason for these precautions. A Ministry of Information spokesman stated on Oct. 10 that there had been an attempted coup and that several officers and civilians had been arrested, but a few minutes later this report was denied in a communiqué issued by the President's office. In a broadcast later the same day President Thieu accused "certain persons" of claiming to have the support of units of the armed forces for "illegal attempts", and gave warning that persons who spread false rumours would be punished. Although he gave no explanation for the state of alert, it was commented that he did not suggest that this was connected with the Viet Cong's activities.

President Thieu signed on Nov. 5 a law prohibiting strikes and public meetings, and providing for the trial of offences against national security by military courts.

Government Measures against the Press

Press censorship was abolished on May 30, 1968, but the Government continued to take severe measures against newspapers publishing material of which it disapproved.

The editor of a student newspaper was sentenced to five years' hard labour on July 25 for publishing news which "leant towards a false peace in favour of the Communists", and the editor of the English-language *Saigon Daily News* was fined 100,000 piastres and given a suspended sentence of three months' imprisonment on Aug. 12 for allegedly misreporting a speech by Tran Van Huong. The leading newspaper *Song* was suspended on Aug. 1 and its editor threatened with prosecution after it had alleged that U.S. military police had looted houses at Cam Ranh while searching for stolen goods. Although this report was denied by the Government and the U.S. military authorities, a committee of the House of Representatives held on Aug. 7 that it was justified, and called on the Government not to prosecute the editor. The House adopted on Aug. 14 a resolution urging the Government to request the U.S. authorities to punish the soldiers responsible for the alleged looting at Cam Ranh and similar incidents elsewhere.

The Minister of Information, Ton That Thien, was strongly criticized in the Press for his wholesale suppression of newspapers, and the *Saigon Post* drew attention to the fact that his Ministry was paying large subsidies to the *Vietnam Guardian,* of which he had previously been editor. Ton That Thien resigned in consequence on Nov. 24, and the Prime Minister on Dec. 2 ordered the payment of the subsidies to be ended. Nguyen Ngoc An took over the Ministry of Information on Dec. 20, while retaining the post of "Open Arms" Minister. The suppression of newspapers nevertheless continued, and a form of indirect censorship was exercised by "requesting" editors to omit certain news items on the ground that they were false. A motion accusing the Government of systematically suppressing the Opposition Press was signed on Feb. 4, 1969, by 61 members of the House of Representatives. [For the "Open Arms" Ministry see page 156.]

A Buddhist weekly was suspended indefinitely on Jan. 28 for publishing material considered likely to weaken the armed forces' morale; a Catholic weekly was suspended for three days on Feb. 9 for criticizing the Supreme Court; and the influential newspaper *Chinh Luan* was suspended on April 17 for reproducing a comment from Hanoi without adding a rebuttal. Three newspapers were suspended on May 20, bringing the number suspended since the lifting of the censorship to 30; one was accused of publishing a rumour that President Nixon had made a secret agreement with the Communists guaranteeing the neutrality of South Vietnam, another of criticizing the conduct of the Americans in Vietnam and the third of printing a caricature of President Thieu.

142

Ly Qui Chung, whose newspaper had recently been suppressed, told the Press on June 28: "The only voice which is allowed to be heard is that of those prepared to fight to the last. Politicians are threatened, newspapers are suppressed. If the Government persists in its attitude it will become completely isolated, and the Opposition will be pushed more and more towards the N.L.F. This has already happened last year; non-Communists, especially students, went over to the other side because they had no other way of participating in the national cause. We do not want to overthrow the Government. We only ask for the right to express a different point of view. . . ."

Assassination of Dr. Le Minh Tri — Attempt on Tran Van Huong

Violence by unidentified assailants led to the death of the Minister of Education and an attempt on the Prime Minister's life early in 1969.

Dr. Le Minh Tri replaced Dr. Nguyen Van Tho as Education Minister in September 1968, after allegations had been made that officials of the Education Ministry were involved in the sale of examination passes. On Jan. 6, 1969, Dr. Tri was assassinated, when a bomb was thrown into his car in a Saigon street from a passing motor-cycle. The police were reported to be investigating whether the crime was the work of Viet Cong terrorists or an act of private revenge; officials stated that as a result of his efforts to end corruption in the examination system Dr. Tri had received many threatening letters. Dr. Tran Anh, professor of medicine at Saigon University and a close political associate of Dr. Tri, was shot dead on March 4, 1969.

An attempt was made to assassinate Tran Van Huong on March 5, when two men fired several shots at his car, and a Claymore mine and 10 lb. of plastic explosive were found hidden under the seat of a pedicab standing nearby. The Prime Minister's spokesman refused to say whether the attack was believed to be the work of the Viet Cong.

Cabinet Changes

The most striking features of new Cabinet appointments, announced on March 12, 1969, were the promotion to Deputy Premier of General Tran Thien Khiem, who had already been appointed Minister for Pacification on March 1, while retaining the Ministry of the Interior, and the appointment of Cao Van Than as Minister of Agriculture *vice* Truong Thai Ton, which removed Vice-President Ky's last supporter from the Cabinet.

Law on Political Parties — Formation of National Social Democratic Front

A Bill on the status of political parties was passed by the House of

143

Representatives on June 11, 1968, and by the Senate on April 28, 1969. This provided that parties must be officially authorized by the Ministry of the Interior, but might oppose the Government, provided this right was exercised "publicly, legally, non-violently and within the framework of serving the country". Members of the armed forces were forbidden to work for political parties. Offences against the law were punishable by five years' imprisonment, and parties might be dissolved if their activities were considered to be directed against the regime.

An organization called the National Salvation Front was formed on Feb. 18, 1968, with the object of uniting pro-Government and anti-Government forces in a single anti-Communist front, its joint chairmen being Lieut.-General Tran Van Don (a prominent Senator), Tran Van Tuyen (a former Vice-Premier), and Tran Quoc Buu (president of the Vietnamese Confederation of Labour). The last-named resigned from the leadership on Feb. 23, however, as a protest against the arrest of his trade union colleagues [see page 134]. Other prominent figures who announced their support for the movement included three of the candidates in the 1967 presidential election—Tran Van Huong, Phan Khac Suu, and Ha Thuc Ky—and Thich Thien Minh. Although the leaders of the Front were of widely differing political and religious views, they had all been known in the past as opponents of President Thieu and Vice-President Ky, and several were opposed to the political influence of the North Vietnamese refugees who were the latter's strongest supporters.

A new party, the Liberal and Democratic Front, was formed on March 27, 1968; its leader, Nguyen Van Huong, was secretary-general of the President's office. After President Thieu had appealed to the political parties on June 29 to form themselves into two main groups, one for and one against the Government, the National Salvation Front, the Liberal and Democratic Front and the Workers' and Peasants' Party (an organization sponsored by the Vietnamese Confederation of Labour) agreed on July 1, 1968, to form the People's Alliance for Social Revolution, with General Tran Van Don as its president.

Addressing both Houses of the National Assembly on April 7, 1969, President Thieu again appealed for the formation of a two-party system, stating that he would form his own political party and that he would

144

welcome the formation of a "constructive Opposition group". This appeal was followed by intensive discussions among the political parties, of which there were over 100, few of them with any wide support. The National Salvation Front withdrew from the People's Alliance for Social Revolution on April 13, as a result of differences over its attitude towards the proposed pro-Government party.

The Greater Vietnam Revolutionary Party, the Socialist Democratic Party and the People's Alliance for Social Revolution, together with seven minor organizations, agreed on April 26, 1969, to form a pro-Government alliance and to hold a convention on May 15, and the alliance was subsequently joined by the Greater Solidarity Force, the Humanist Socialist Party and the Vietnamese Nationalist Party. Many differences of opinion arose during the negotiations between the leaders of these parties and President Thieu, however; in particular, all the parties except the People's Alliance insisted that Nguyen Van Huong, who was regarded as the President's agent, must play no part in the leadership of the new alliance.

The inaugural convention of the alliance, which adopted the name of the National Social Democratic Front, took place in Saigon on May 25, 1969, and was attended by 1,500 delegates. Addressing the convention, President Thieu said that the Front would not be "totalitarian or despotic", and that it would "do everything possible to prevent a hasty peace solution in Paris and to prevent the country from falling into the hands of the Communists". Much comment was aroused by the fact that neither Vice-President Ky nor Tran Van Huong was present at the convention. [For Paris peace talks see note on page 151.]

Of the six major parties forming the Front—described by the *New York Times* as "essentially a grouping of largely conservative organizations of centrists and Roman Catholic refugees from North Vietnam that would probably support President Thieu even in the absence of the new alliance"—the **Greater Vietnam Revolutionary Party**, led by Ha Thuc Ky, was one of the three factions into which the right-wing Greater Vietnam Party (Dai Viet) had split, the other two being the Neo Dai Viet and the "Dai Viet Veterans". The **Socialist Democratic Party** was a faction of the Hoa Hao sect. The **Greater Solidarity Force** was an extreme right-wing organization of Catholic refugees, led by Senator Nguyen Gia Hien. The **Humanist Socialist Party** consisted of former members of the Can Lao, the only legal party under President Ngo Dinh Diem's regime. The **Vietnamese Nationalist Party** (Vietnam Quoc Dan Dang) was the oldest non-Communist party in Vietnam, and was formed in the 1920s as an anti-French party modelled on the Chinese Kuomintang. In addition to the National Salvation Front, several important political and religious groups remained outside the National Social Democratic Front, including the militant Buddhists, the moderate Catholics, the Caodaists and a section of the Hoa Hao.

Opposition Movements

A new Opposition party, the Progressive Nationalist Movement, was formed on April 20, 1969, under the leadership of Dr. Nguyen Ngoc Huy, a member of the South Vietnamese delegation to the Paris peace talks, who as leader of the Neo Dai Viet had actively supported Truong Dinh Dzu in the 1967 presidential election. Its manifesto, while blaming "Communists and colonialists" for South Vietnam's troubles, also denounced "feudal and reactionary elements who flock together behind a façade of anti-Communism in order to exploit their fellow-countrymen". A number of leading Opposition politicians, including General Tran Van Don, Dr. Nguyen Ngoc Huy, Phan Khac Suu and representatives of the militant Buddhists, met in Saigon on June 15 to discuss the possibility of uniting the anti-Government parties into a "third force".

Duong Van Minh claimed on Nov. 13, 1969, that a majority of the Vietnamese population supported neither the Thieu regime nor the National Liberation Front but wanted peace, independence and neutrality, and he began to organize a "Third Force" movement which was to represent this majority.

President Thieu, in a speech made in Vung Tau on Dec. 9, referred to the followers of the "Third Force" movement as "imbeciles" and to certain deputies as "Communist dogs".

His remarks, however, were rejected by a group of sixteen deputies as being "irresponsible" and revealing his dictatorial tendencies.

XI. ACTIVITIES OF THE NATIONAL LIBERATION FRONT — 1968-69

Alliance of National, Democratic and Peace Forces

The Alliance of National, Democratic and Peace Forces, the formation of which had been announced by the N.L.F. radio during the Tet offensive, elected its leadership at a secret conference held on April 20-21, 1968, in N.L.F.-controlled territory claimed to be near Saigon. A communiqué issued by the conference said that the aims of the Alliance were to "re-establish peace, recover independence and national sovereignty, build up South Vietnam as an independent, free, peaceful, neutral and prosperous State, and move towards reunification of the country through discussions and negotiations between the South and the North on a basis of equality", and that the conference had decided in favour of unity of action with the N.L.F.

The members of the Alliance's central committee elected by the conference were—*Chairman:* Trinh Dinh Thao, a Saigon lawyer who had acted as Minister of Justice during the Japanese occupation in 1945. *Vice-chairmen:* Lam Van Tet, an engineer and a member of the "Council of Notabilities" set up after the overthrow of President Ngo Dinh Diem [see page 48], and Thich Don Hau, a leader of the militant Buddhist movement who had taken a prominent part in the Hué revolt of 1966. *General Secretary:* Professor Ton That Duong Ky, a member of the former Imperial family who was expelled to North Vietnam in 1965 for supporting an appeal for peace [see page 83]. *Assistant General Secretaries:* Mme. Duong Quynh Hao, a

147

doctor, Hoang Trong, a writer better known by his pen-name "Thanh Nghi" and Le Hieu Dang, described as a student. *Other Members:* Tran Lieu Luat, a teacher, Professor Nguyen Van Kiet, a former professor of French literature at Saigon University, and Huynh Van Nghi.

The 10 members of the central committee were condemned to death and confiscation of their property *in absentia* by a South Vietnamese military court on July 12, on charges of treason and "working for the Communists under the cover of appeals for peace and neutrality"

At a second conference on July 30-31, 1968, also claimed to have been held near Saigon, the Alliance adopted its political programme, which called for absolute respect for the fundamental clauses of the Geneva Agreements, i.e. the independence, sovereignty, and territorial integrity of Vietnam, the withdrawal of all foreign troops, and the dismantling of all foreign bases, and stated that the Alliance was prepared to enter into discussions with the U.S. Government on these questions. The programme also proposed the formation of "a broad, national and democratic Government"; the dissolution of the National Assembly; the annulment of the 1967 Constitution; a foreign policy based on "non-alignment with any camp or bloc and non-participation in any alliance whatsoever"; a "just and reasonable" programme of agrarian reform; and an economic policy of "freedom for enterprises profitable to the State and the people"

Provisional Government Formed by N.L.F. and Alliance of National, Democratic and Peace Forces

The N.L.F. announced on June 10, 1969, that a "Provisional Revolutionary Government of the Republic of Vietnam" had been established. This development completed the process of setting up a system of government in the areas controlled by the N.L.F., which had been in progress since the offensive of February 1968.

Since 1966 the N.L.F.'s official policy had been to discourage the establishment of "government-style rural administrative councils" in order that "the basic revolutionary machinery will not be complicated", and the administration of the villages under its control had been left to the local branches of the People's Revolutionary (Communist) Party, which collected taxes, administered justice and carried out land redistribution. The first intimation of a change of policy was the establishment of a Revolutionary Committee for Thua Thien province on Feb. 14, 1968, during the temporary occupation of Hué by the Viet Cong. "People's Liberation Councils" of 15 to 35 members, according to the size of the village, were elected in June and July in villages controlled by the N.L.F., and in turn elected "People's Liberation Committees" of five to seven members in charge of both military and administrative affairs; in disputed areas non-elective village councils were set up. Although exact details were not known, according to foreign correspondents'

148

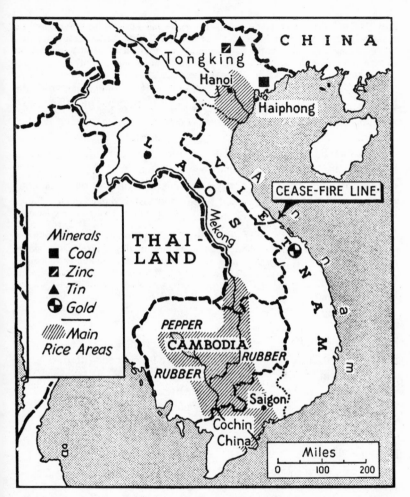

Indo-China, showing economic resources and the cease-fire line in Vietnam. The shaded area around Hanoi corresponds approximately to the Red River Delta.

(*Economist*)

dispatches it was believed that elections had taken place in nearly 2,000 hamlets out of the 14,000 in South Vietnam, and that about 1,000,000 people had taken part in them. During the later months of 1968 and the first half of 1969 Revolutionary Committees were established in the provinces and a number of larger towns, culminating in the formation of an underground Revolutionary Committee for Saigon and Cholon on May 30, 1969. On July 31, *Le Monde* reported that Revolutionary Committees were apparently in existence in all provinces in South Vietnam with the exception of Binh Tuy, Phuoc Than, Hau Nghia, Go Cong, Vinh Binh, An Giang, Chuon Thien, Phu Quoc and Con Son.

The N.L.F. radio announced on June 10 that the "Provisional Revolutionary Government" had been elected at a congress of 88 representatives of political parties, national minorities, religious communities, social classes, the armed forces, and youth organizations, which had been convened jointly by the N.L.F. and the Alliance of National, Democratic and Peace Forces and had been held on June 6-8; the location of the meeting was not mentioned. The membership of the Provisional Government was given as follows:

Huynh Tan Phat	Prime Minister.
Professor Nguyen Van Kiet	Deputy Premier and Education and Youth.
Nguyen Doan	Deputy Premier.
Dr. Phung Van Cung	Deputy Premier and Interior.
Tran Buu Kiem	Minister in the Prime Minister's Office.
Tran Nam Trung	Defence.
Mme. Nguyen Thi Binh	Foreign Affairs.
Cao Van Bon	Economy and Finance.
Lieu Huu Phuoc	Information and Culture.
Mme. Duong Quynh Hao	Health and Social Affairs.
Truong Nhu Tang	Justice.

There were also 13 Deputy Ministers.

Huynh Tan Phat became engaged in nationalist activities in 1936, and as leader of the Democratic Party, of which he was general secretary, took an active part in the war against the French, becoming head of the Vietminh information service. After practising as an architect in Saigon he went underground in 1958, when President Ngo Dinh Diem suppressed the Opposition parties, and joined the N.L.F. on its formation in 1960. Of the Deputy Premiers, **Professor Nguyen Van Kiet** and **Nguyen Doan** were leading members of the Alliance, and **Dr. Phung Van Cung**, a medical

150

practitioner in Saigon before going underground in 1960, was vice-chairman of the N.L.F. and head of its health services.

Tran Buu Kiem, a lawyer, took part in nationalist activities during the Second World War, in the uprising of 1945, and in the subsequent war against the French. A member of the presidium of the N.L.F., he was responsible for its foreign relations and headed the N.L.F. delegation at the Paris peace talks.* He was a leading member of the Democratic Party.

Mme. Nguyen Thi Binh was arrested in 1951 for anti-French activities and imprisoned for three years. As a member of the N.L.F. central committee she led many delegations to foreign countries. On her appointment as Foreign Minister she succeeded Tran Buu Kiem as leader of the N.L.F. delegation at the Paris peace talks, of which she was already a member.

Little was known of the other members of the Provisional Government. The *New York Times* Correspondent in Hong Kong described **Tran Nam Trung** as general secretary of the People's Revolutionary (Communist) Party, but both the *Times* Correspondent in Paris and *Le Monde* reported that none of the leading members of the Provisional Government was known to be a Communist.

An advisory committee of seven members of the N.L.F. and six members of the Alliance was appointed to assist the Provisional Government. It was headed by Nguyen Huu Tho, chairman of the N.L.F., and Trinh Dinh Thao, chairman of the Alliance, and also included the two vice-chairmen of the Alliance, Lam Van Tet and Thich Don Hau, and representatives of the Catholic, Caodaist, Montagnard and Khmer communities. [The Khmers are one of the major ethnic groups in South-East Asia, forming the majority of the population in Cambodia and a minority in Vietnam.]

The "Provisional Revolutionary Government" adopted the following 12-point programme of action:

(1) To compel the U.S. Government to withdraw its forces totally and unconditionally from South Vietnam.

(2) "To abolish the disguised colonial regime established by the U.S. imperialists in South Vietnam, to overthrow the entire structure of the puppet administration, to

---

*The Paris peace talks were opened on May 13, 1968, between North Vietnam and the United States. The object of these discussions was defined by the North Vietnamese Government as "being to agree on the unconditional cessation of the bombing and of all other U.S. acts of war against the Democratic Republic of Vietnam", whilst President Johnson expressed the hope that the discussions would "represent a mutual and serious movement by all parties towards peace in South-East Asia".

Delegations from South Vietnam and the National Liberation Front were admitted to the talks after October 1968.

abolish the Constitution and all anti-national and anti-democratic laws enacted by the puppet administration, . . . to build a really democratic and free republican regime, and to organize general elections. . .without foreign interference."

(3) To enter into consultations with "the political forces representing the various social strata and political tendencies in South Vietnam that stand for peace, independence and neutrality", with a view to setting up a provisional coalition Government which would organize elections to a Constituent Assembly, work out a democratic Constitution, and set up "a coalition Government reflecting national concord and a broad union of all social strata".

(4) To build up the revolutionary armed forces and consolidate and widen the "liberated zone".

(5) "To achieve broad democratic freedoms, . . . to prohibit all acts of repression, reprisal and discrimination against people having collaborated with either side, . . . to achieve equality between men and women in all fields, to carry out a policy of unity and equality among the various nationalities, . . . to respect freedom of belief, and to achieve equality among the various religions."

(6) To improve the living conditions of the workers, fix minimum wages, and guarantee the right of workers to take part in the management of enterprises and to join trade unions. Educational opportunities would be guaranteed to the young, freedom of thought, opinion and the press to the intellectuals, and freedom of enterprise to industrialists and traders.

(7) To restore and develop agricultural and industrial production and create conditions for the building of a self-supporting economy. The right of ownership of the means of production and other property would be protected.

(8) To develop education, science and technology, liquidate illiteracy, and develop the health services.

(9) To welcome and reward soldiers and officials of the "puppet administration" who "cross over to the side of the people" and to "refrain from any discrimination against those guilty persons who repent and truly rejoin the ranks of the people".

(10) To assist war invalids and the families of those killed on both sides, and to solve the unemployment problem.

(11) To re-establish normal relations between South and North Vietnam, guarantee freedom of movement, correspondence and residence, and maintain economic and cultural relations between them. The reunification of the country would be achieved "step by step, by peaceful means, through discussions and agreement between the two zones, without constraint from either side".

(12) To carry out a foreign policy of peace and neutrality; to pursue a good-neighbour policy with Cambodia and Laos; to establish diplomatic, economic and cultural relations with all countries, irrespective of their political and social regimes, including the United States, in accordance with the five principles of peaceful co-existence; to accept aid, with no political conditions attached, from any country; to refrain from joining any military alliance; not to allow any foreign country to maintain military bases or troops in South Vietnam; and not to recognize the protection of any country or military alliance.

The first country to recognize the Provisional Revolutionary Government was Cuba, whose Ambassador to Cambodia had already been accredited to the N.L.F. in March. It was also recognized on June 11 by Algeria; on June 12 by North Korea and Syria; on June 13 by North

152

Vietnam, Cambodia, the Soviet Union, Rumania, Bulgaria, Eastern Germany, Poland, Yugoslavia, Hungary, Czechoslovakia, Outer Mongolia, and Congo (Brazzaville); on June 14 by China; on June 15 by South Yemen; in the next four days by Albania, Mauritania, and the Sudan; on July 10 by Iraq; and on July 12 by the United Arab Republic.

President Thieu described the establishment of the Provisional Government on June 11 as "a propaganda trick", and asked: "Of what value are Governments formed by men hidden in the jungles and mountains who do not even dare to reveal the place where their Government is established?" A State Department spokesman in Washington on the same day described the new Government as "the same old wine in a new bottle" and other U.S. officials claimed that all the ministers in the new organization were either members of the N.L.F. or "sleepers", i.e. agents of the Front "masquerading as members of the Alliance".

In an official communiqué on talks between Premier Chou En-lai and Nguyen Huu Tho issued on October 15, 1969, the N.L.F. and the Provisional Revolutionary Government thanked the Chinese Government and people for "the powerful support and the great, sincere and effective assistance. . . which they have consistently given to the people of Southern Vietnam in the latter's war against U.S. aggression".

XII. CONSOLIDATION OF PRESIDENT THIEU'S REGIME

Cabinet Formed by General Tran Thien Khiem

A South Vietnamese Government spokesman stated on July 18 that major Cabinet changes would be announced within the next few days, but that the Prime Minister, Tran Van Huong, had no intention of resigning. The Ministry of Information announced on July 21 that all the members of the Government had tendered their resignation in order to allow Tran Van Huong to carry out the proposed reshuffle; after several Ministers had denied that they had resigned, however, the statement was withdrawn.

A majority of the House of Representatives had previously demanded Tran Van Huong's resignation on July 2. Discontent with the Government was caused largely by recent increases in taxation and its failure to curb inflation, the *Financial Times* correspondent in Saigon quoting on Aug. 24 a review of South Vietnam's economic situation by the U.S. Agency for International Development which showed that the cost of living had increased by 23 per cent in the past 3½ months.

The leaders of the parties constituting the National Social Democratic Front (the six-party alliance sponsored by President Nguyen Van Thieu) demanded on Aug. 8 the dismissal of Tran Van Huong and the appointment of a new Prime Minister to "raise the country's prestige". After prolonged negotiations, it was officially announced on Aug. 22 that

154

"in order to meet the political need and not to let the current national situation drag on any longer, Prime Minister Tran Van Huong has agreed that President Nguyen Van Thieu will choose another person to form a new Cabinet". According to unofficial sources, the President and the Prime Minister had failed to agree on the Cabinet changes because the former wished to broaden the Government by including representatives of all the non-Communist political parties, whereas the latter had wished to form a Government of technicians without party ties.

President Thieu asked the Deputy Prime Minister, General Tran Thien Khiem, on Aug. 23 to form a Government. General Khiem's appointment was reported to have been sponsored by a group of retired generals headed by Vice-President Nguyen Cao Ky, but to have been opposed by the U.S. Ambassador, Mr. Ellsworth Bunker, who considered it undesirable that the President, Vice-President, and Prime Minister should all be military officers.

Attempts by General Khiem to broaden the basis of the Government met with no success, as several prominent political figures declined invitations to take office. These included leaders of the two largest parties in the National Social Democratic Front, Ha Thuc Ky, of the Greater Vietnam Revolutionary Party, and Tran Van Tuyen, of the Vietnamese Nationalist Party; Lieut.-General Tran Van Don, leader of the National Salvation Front; Nguyen Van Bong, a leader of the Progressive Nationalist Movement; and Au Truong Thanh, a former Minister for the Economy and Finance, who for the past year had lived in Paris. As a result of the politicians' refusal to co-operate with him, General Khiem was forced to form a Government consisting largely of soldiers, civil servants, and technicians.

The membership of the new Government was announced on Sept. 1 as follows:

General Tran Thien Khiem	Prime Minister and Interior.
Dr. Nguyen Luu Vien	Deputy Premier and Education.
Mai Tho Truyen	Minister of State for Cultural Affairs.
Professor Vu Quoc Thuc	Minister of State for Reconstruction and Development.

155

Dr. Nguyen Tien Hy	Ministers of State.
Dr. Phan Quang Dan	
Tran Van Lam	Foreign Affairs.
Lieut.-General Nguyen Van Vy	Defence.
Le Van Thu	Justice.
Pham Kim Ngoc	Economy.
Nguyen Bich Hue	Finance.
Major-General Tran Thanh Phong	Revolutionary Development.
Ngo Khac Tinh	Information.
Dr. Ho Van Cham	"Open Arms."†
Cao Van Than	Land Reform, Agriculture and Fisheries.
Duong Kich Nhuong	Public Works.
Tran Van Vien	Transport and Posts.
Dr. Tran Minh Tung	Health.
Dr. Tran Nguon Phieu	Social Welfare.
Dam Sy Hien	Labour.
Major-General Pham Van Dong	Ex-servicemen.
Paul Nur	Ethnic Development.
Nguyen Van Vang	Secretary of State at Prime Minister's Office.
Cao Van Tuong	Secretary of State for Liaison with National Assembly.

†The Ministry of Open Arms *(Chieu Hoi)* is responsible for the Government's programme for bringing about the surrender of Viet Cong supporters.

There were also seven Deputy Ministers.

The new Government was widely criticized in South Vietnamese political circles as unrepresentative and as containing too many military men and former Diemists. The Progressive Nationalist Movement asserted on Sept. 2 that it "represents nobody" and could only make the prospect of peace more distant, whilst Tran Van Tuyen said that it had "too many people, too many technicians, and no political nature"

Trial of North Vietnamese Agents and South Vietnamese Intellectuals

Police spokesmen announced at a press conference in Saigon on April 17, 1969, that 26 doctors, university teachers, writers, publishers, and other intellectuals had been arrested on charges of having been in contact with North Vietnamese agents. Among those arrested was Nguyen Lau, the owner-editor of the English-language *Saigon Daily News,* who read a statement at the press conference admitting that he had had several meetings with a North Vietnamese agent, Captain Tran Ngoc Hien, whom he had known since childhood, and had failed to denounce him. A political sensation was caused when Tran Ngoc Chau, secretary-general of the House of Representatives, revealed on April 23 that Captain Hien was his brother.

Tran Ngoc Chau, who was a leader of the pro-Government group in the House of Representatives and was regarded as a close political associate of President Thieu, had previously put forward a peace plan in an interview with *Le Monde* on Jan. 16. Since a military victory was "impossible" and defeat "inconceivable", he said, it was necessary to recognize the existence of the N.L.F. and to enter into direct negotiations with it. After a cease-fire had been negotiated, the N.L.F. should be invited to nominate representatives to the National Assembly, on condition that they were not "notorious Communists". A coalition Government should then be formed, in which a minority of the members would be N.L.F. representatives. N.L.F. members should take part in the next elections to the Assembly, whether as individuals or as representatives of the Front, and finally the North and South Vietnamese Governments should discuss the reunification of the country.

Captain Hien, Mme. Paulette Quoi (another North Vietnamese agent), Nguyen Lau, Vo Dinh Cuong (a militant Buddhist leader and a cousin of Captain Hien), and 18 others were tried by a military court on July 4. At the trial Nguyen Lau repudiated the statement which he had read at the press conference, claiming that he had signed it under pressure while in prison and that when he had met Captain Hien he had not known that he was a North Vietnamese agent. Captain Hien was sentenced to hard labour for life, Mme. Quoi to 20 years' hard labour, Nguyen Lau and Vo Dinh Cuong to five years' imprisonment, and 13 others to various terms of imprisonment. Five of the accused were acquitted.

Tran Ngoc Chau revealed on the same day that he had himself had a series of meetings with his brother in an attempt to bring about a peace settlement. He refused to say whether or not President Thieu or the Americans had been aware of his initiatives, saying that he must remain silent on this point as "a matter of honour".

Tran Ngoc Chau said that in April 1968 he had proposed to his brother that a delegation from the National Assembly, including himself, should visit Hanoi in order to bring about discussions between North and South Vietnam. Captain Hien had informed him in the following June that the North Vietnamese Government was prepared to meet such a delegation either in Hanoi or in Laos, but only as individuals and not in an official capacity. In August he had submitted to the Assembly a petition signed by many of its members in favour of direct negotiations with Hanoi. As the Assembly, although "hesitant," had not rejected this proposal, he had asked Captain Hien whether the North Vietnamese Government would receive a delegation which included both deputies and leading political figures, and had emphasized that such a delegation must be accepted as representatives of the South Vietnamese people. Three weeks later Captain Hien had told him that Hanoi maintained its previous position, but that if the delegation brought new proposals they might be recognized as an official delegation. He had therefore drawn up his peace plan, but when this was published in January 1969 it had had such an unfavourable reception in Saigon that he had taken no further steps before his brother was arrested.

Tran Ngoc Chau and Huynh Van Tu Accused of
Pro-Communist Activities – Their Trial and Imprisonment

In November 1969 President Thieu submitted to the House of Representatives dossiers accusing two members—Pham The Truc and Huynh Van Tu—of having affiliations with the Communists. The former had, in Tokyo in May 1969, publicly called for the establishment of a coalition Government in South Vietnam and demanded the withdrawal of all U.S. troops, and the latter was accused of belonging to a spy network directed by Huynh Van Trong, special assistant to President Thieu.

The Government, however, repeatedly failed in its attempts to obtain parliamentary approval for the prosecution of Pham The Truc, Tran Ngoc Chau and Huynh Van Tu all of whom had been charged with Communist affiliations in a report by a special investigating committee. The House of Representatives agreed on Dec. 31 to the charges but refused to lift the three members' parliamentary immunity.

Demonstrations against the presence of Huynh Van Tu and Pham The Truc in the House of Representatives took place on Dec. 20-22, 1969, in Vung Tau, Kien Phong, Bien Hoa and Saigon, where a group of demonstrators forcibly entered the House of Representatives.

158

This invasion of Parliament was strongly condemned by Opposition members who, on Dec. 23 accused the President of making preparations for the establishment of a dictatorship, while half the members present in the Senate considered the President to be responsible for the demonstrations. The National Salvation Front protested on Dec. 27 against the invasion of the House of Representatives and condemned "provocative statements" made by President Thieu, who had accused the "Third Force" movement of being pro-Communist. A senatorial commission accused the President on Jan. 6, 1970, of having contributed to the organization of the demonstrations in the House of Representatives.

The National Assembly, however, decided on Feb. 4 by the required three-quarters majority to lift the parliamentary immunity of Tran Ngoc Chau and also of Huynh Van Tu, but not that of Pham The Truc.

A Military Court in Saigon, at a session lasting only 30 minutes on Feb. 25, sentenced Huynh Van Tu—who had meanwhile fled the country—to death for high treason, and Tran Ngoc Chau to 20 years' hard labour for anti-Government activities. The latter had previously been in hiding for three weeks until Feb. 23, when he reappeared in the House of Representatives, stating that he would remain there until after his trial. He was arrested in the House on Feb. 26.

Following an appeal, Tran Ngoc Chau was retried on March 2-5, 1970. The defendant did not deny that he had met his brother eight times between 1965 and 1969 but claimed that leading U.S. officials had been aware of his contacts which were made in an effort to ease the way to a negotiated settlement of the war. He repeated that he was an anti-Communist Nationalist. The court, however, found him guilty on the charges concerning the eight visits to his brother but reduced the previous sentence to 10 years' hard labour.

Land Reform

A Land Reform Bill, approved by the House of Representatives on Sept. 9, 1969, provided for the transfer of, within two years, 1,300,000,000 hectares of land into ownership by the 800,000 peasants working on it. Under the Bill every peasant would, within 30 days after its

159

adoption by Parliament, receive the title deeds of his land, exemption from land tax for one year and credits for the purchase of equipment and fertilizer.

The project to be implemented by the Bill had been decided upon by Presidents Thieu and Nixon at their meeting on Midway Island on June 8, 1969, as part of South Vietnam's social revolution by which all people would be given an equal opportunity and productivity would be increased.

The details of the programme had first been explained by Cao Van Than (the Minister of Agriculture) on June 20 and 23, 1969.

He said that during 1969 the Government would complete the distribution of 147,221 hectares of land which had either been expropriated under an ordinance promulgated by President Ngo Dinh Diem in 1956, limiting ownership of rice-lands to 100 hectares, or been purchased from French citizens in the late 1950s with financial help received from France. Little of the land then acquired had been distributed before July 1968, when the Government had set in motion an accelerated distribution campaign, and the 140,000 hectares scheduled for 1969 represented virtually all of the remaining Government-owned land which was cultivated. [A report submitted to the U.S. State Department in December 1967 by two members of the House of Representatives, Mr. John Moss (Democrat) and Mr. Ogden Reid (Republican), stated that of 1,025,000 hectares acquired by the Government since 1954 only 330,000 hectares had so far been distributed among the peasantry. Much of the remaining land, it was stated in press reports, had been allowed to pass out of cultivation.]

Turning to the Bill, he said that it was intended that title would be given free of charge to all persons now tilling rice-lands, whether as tenants, share-croppers, squatters or cultivators appointed by the Viet Cong, and these farmers, whether or not they had contracts, would be encouraged to make application for ownership, the landlords being compensated by the Government. Farmers tilling communal land or land belonging to religious authorities would similarly receive a title; religious authorities would be compensated like expropriated landlords, and villages losing communal lands would receive limited compensation.

Titles would be issued by the village administrative committees, to whom the farmers benefiting from the scheme would pay their land tax (beginning one year after receiving title to the land), and ownership would be registered with the provincial authorities and the central Government. Compensation to the landlords would be 20 per cent in cash and 80 per cent in negotiable eight-year Government bonds bearing interest and being linked to the price of paddy. The price of the land would be determined by local officials according to guidelines issued by the Government, based on the average yield during the past five years.

He said that the programme was "an important and decisive factor in the military and political struggle between the Government of Vietnam and the Communists"; would overcome the reluctance of farmers to pay taxes to the central Government; and could be speedily implemented through the use of simplified procedures and aerial photographs. Its implementation would be supervised by the

President himself, who in the forthcoming legislation would be granted authority to work out details of the reform, based on the general principles laid down in the Bill. Under directives issued by the Prime Minister on Feb. 12 and April 25, 1969, current land occupancy and rents had already been frozen for one year, so that no farmer could be evicted by the legal owner or the Government, nor could he be asked to pay a higher rent. If 80 per cent of the farmers responded to the new programme, compensation payable by the Government would cover over 1,000,000 acres.

Under one of two agreements signed in Saigon on June 27, the U.S.A. granted $10,000,000 in aid towards the implementation of the land reform programme.

(Sources: South Vietnamese Embassy Press Department, London – Vietnam Press Agency, Saigon – U.S. Information Service – *New York Times* – *New York Herald Tribune* – International Control Commission, Special Report, Cmnd.1755 (H.M.S.O., London) – *Times*, London – *Daily Telegraph*, London – *Manchester Guardian* – *Guardian*, London – *Financial Times*, London – *Observer*, London – *Le Monde*, Paris – *Le Figaro*, Paris – *Neue Zürcher Zeitung* – *Peking Review*).

PERSONALITIES
[Figures represent page numbers]

Au Truong Thanh—115, 125, 134, 155
Minister for Economic Affairs 1963-66.
Bacut, General—11-12, 15-16
Leader of Hoa Hao forces 1955.
Bao Dai, Emperor—2-6, 10, 13-15, 17
Head of State, [South] Vietnam 1945, 1949 - 1955.
Bunker, Ellsworth—125, 155
U.S. Ambassador in South Vietnam March 1967- .
Buu Loc Prince—3-5
Prime Minister, [South] Vietnam 1953-54.
Cao Van Than—143, 156, 160
Minister for Agriculture, Land Reform and Fisheries 1969- .
Cao Van Vien—63, 83, 117, 139
Chief of Staff 1964 -; member of "Young Turks" Movement; member of Committee for the Direction of the State 1965; Defence Minister 1967.
Dam Sy Hien—156
Minister for Labour 1964, 1968 -.
Do Mau—49-50, 60
Vice-Premier 1964.
Don Hau, Thich—147, 151
Vice-Chairman, Alliance of National, Democratic and Peace Forces' Central Committee 1968 -.
Duong Hieu Nghia—61-63, 80
Supporter of attempted coups September 1964 and February 1965.
Duong Ngoc Lam—61-63
Prefect of Saigon 1964; involved in attempted coup September 1964.
Duong Quynh Hao, Mme.—147, 150
Assistant General Secretary, Alliance of National, Democratic and

162

Peace Forces' Central Committee 1968; Minister for Health and Social Affairs (Provisional Revolutionary Government) 1969 -.

Duong Van Duc—61-63
Leader of attempted coup September 1964.

Duong Van Minh—45-49, 54-55, 58, 60-64, 75, 82, 124, 146
Leader of coup November 1963; Chief of State November 1963 - January 1965; in exile 1965-1968; leader of Third Force Movement 1969.

Ha Thuc Ky—53, 145, 155
Leader, Greater Vietnam Revolutionary Party 1968.

Ho Giac, Thich—90-91, 95, 101
Chairman, Struggle Movement Committee 1966.

Huynh Tan Phat—150
Prime Minister (Provisional Revolutionary Government) 1969 -.

Huynh Van Ton—61, 80-81
Involved in attempted coups September 1964 and February 1965.

Huynh Van Tu—158-159
Deputy in House of Representatives accused of pro-Communist activities December 1969.

Lam Van Phat—53, 60-61, 80-81
Minister of Interior April-September 1964; involved in attempted coups September 1964 and February 1965.

Lam Van Tet—147, 151
Vice-chairman, Alliance of National, Democratic and Peace Forces' Central Committee 1968.

Le Van Kim—48-49, 61
General Secretary, Central Executive Committee November 1963; Chief of Staff January 1964.

Le Van Thu—66, 76, 156
Chairman, High National Council November - December 1964; Minister of Justice 1968 -.

Le Van Ty—14, 28, 42
Chief of Staff 1955 - 1963.

Lodge Henry Cabot—46, 50, 89, 99
U.S. Ambassador in Vietnam June 1963 - June 1964, August 1965 - March 1967.

Ngo Dinh Diem—10-25, 29-46
Minister of the Interior in Bao Dai's Government in Annam 1933; resigned in same year; thereafter refused all invitations to accept office, including offers from Japanese occupation authorities in 1945, from Ho Chi Minh in 1946 and from the French Commissioner-General in 1947; in exile in U.S. and Paris 1949-1954; Prime Minister, South Vietnam 1954; President of South Vietnam 1955 - 63; assassinated November 1963.

163

Nguyen Van Loc–132, 138, 10
Prime Minister 1967-68.
Nguyen Van Man–91-92, 99
Mayor of Danang 1966.
Nguyen Van Thieu–50, 62-63, 77, 79, 83, 85-87, 97 100-102, 113, 117-118, 124-130, 133, 135-146, 153-161
Vietminh youth leader 1945-46; left movement on becoming aware of its Communist aims 1946; served with French forces against Vietminh 1946-1954; under Diem's regime, Superintendent of Military Academy and subsequently commander of 5th Infantry Division; Chief of Staff and then commander of 4th Army Corps 1964; Deputy Premier and Defence Minister February 1965; chairman of Committee for the Direction of the State and acting Chief of State June 1965; President of South Vietnam October 1967 -.
Nguyen Van Truong–75, 114-115
Minister of Education 1964 - 66.
Nguyen Van Vy–13-14, 49, 61, 64, 139, 156
Inspector General of Army 1955; Deputy Chief of Staff 1964; Chief of Nguyen Khanh's personal staff 1964; Minister of Defence 1967 -.
Nguyen Xuan Oanh–79
Vice-premier February 1964; Acting Premier August 1964; 2nd Vice-premier November 1964; Acting Prime Minister January 1965.
Nhan Minh Trang–61, 80
Involved in attempted coups September 1964 and February 1965.
Nur Paul–88, 156
Special Commissioner for Montagnard Affairs 1965; Minister for Ethnic Development 1967 -.
Pham Ngoc Thao–80-81
Leader of attempted coup February 1965.
Pham The Truc–158-159
Deputy in House of Representatives accused of pro-Communist activities December 1969.
Pham Van Dong–74, 83-84, 156
Military Governor Saigon 1964; member of Governing Committee of Armed Forces Council 1965; minister for Ex-servicemen 1969-.
Pham Xuan Chieu–50, 80, 92
Vice-chairman of Executive Committee 1964; chairman of National Legislative Council 1965; member of Committee for the Direction of the State 1965; General Secretary of this Committee 1966.
Phan Huy Quat–52, 79, 83-85
Minister for Foreign Affairs 1964; Prime Minister 1965.
Phan Khac Suu–26-27, 41, 64-66, 74-79, 82, 85-86, 111-113, 125-128, 132
Minister of Agriculture 1954; member of Democratic Bloc 1959; member of Committee for Progress and Liberty 1960; chairman, High

National Council 1964; President 1964-65; President of Assembly 1966.

Phan Quang Dan—26, 28-29, 41, 156
Leader of Democratic Bloc 1959; member of Revolutionary Committee 1960; leader of Free Democratic Party 1963; Minister of State 1968 -.

Phan Van Khoa—104-105
Mayor of Hué 1966.

Phan Xuan Nhuan—93, 104-106
Local commander in Hué April - June 1966.

Phung Van Cung—150
Deputy Premier (Provisional Revolutionary Government) 1969-.

Quang Duc, Thich—40, 54, 78
Suicide by fire 1963.

Tam Chau, Thich—56, 74, 90-92, 99-104, 106-107
Director of Vien Hoa Dao (Buddhist Institute); leader of moderate Buddhist faction 1966; chairman of Committee for the Protection of Buddhism 1966.

Taylor, Maxwell D.—33, 45, 55, 57, 59, 63, 70-71, 76, 85-86
Special Military adviser to President Kennedy 1961; chairman, Joint Chiefs of Staff 1963-4; U.S. Ambassador to South Vietnam June 1964 - August 1965.

Thien Minh, Thich—90, 92, 99-102, 135-136, 144
Commissioner for Youth affairs of Vien Hoa Dao 1966; chairman of Struggle Movement Committee 1966.

Tinh Khiet, Thich—37, 41, 43, 89, 103-104, 135
Head of Vietnamese Buddhist Community 1963-.

Ton That Dinh—42-43, 48-49, 61, 64, 94, 106
Military Governor of Saigon 1963; Minister for Security and 2nd Vice-chairman, Central Executive Committee 1963; Assistant to Deputy C.-in-C. 1964; Commander of 1st Army Corps April 1966.

Ton That Duong Ky—83, 148
General Secretary, Alliance of National, Democratic and Peace Forces' Central Committee 1968.

Tran Ngoc Chau—157-159
Secretary-General of House of Representatives 1968-1970; charged with pro-Communist activities December 1969.

Tran Ngoc Lieng—114-115, 124-125
Minister for Social Affairs 1966.

Tran Quoc Buu—64, 144
President, Vietnamese Confederation of Labour 1964; chairman, National Salvation Front 1968.

Tran Thien Khiem—49-50, 55, 58, 60-62, 81-82, 143, 155
Crushed attempted coup November 1960; involved in successful coups November 1963 and January 1964 (leader); Defence Minister and

166

C.-in-C. 1964; virtual exile in October 1964 when appointed South Vietnamese Ambassador to U.S. and subsequently in October 1965 Ambassador to Formosa; Minister of the Interior May 1968 -; Deputy Premier March 1969; Prime Minister August 1969-.

Tran Van An–20, 50
Minister of Information 1948-49 (General Van Xuan's Provisional Government); Minister of "Open Arms" 1965; member of Committee for the Direction of the State 1966.

Tran Van Do–6, 8, 11, 27, 41
Minister for Foreign Affairs 1954; member of Committee for Progress and Liberty 1960; Deputy Premier and Minister for Foreign Affairs February 1965; Minister for Foreign Affairs June 1965; Member of Committee for the Direction of the State 1966; Minister for Foreign Affairs 1966-69.

Tran Van Don–42, 48-49, 61, 64, 144, 146, 155
Chief of Staff 1963; Minister for Defence November 1963-January 1964; Deputy C.-in-C. November 1964; Chairman, National Salvation Front 1968 -.

Tran Van Huong–61, 66, 71, 74, 76-79, 127, 137, 138, 140, 142, 144, 154-155
Prefect of Saigon 1964; Prime Minister and Minister for Defence November 1964 - January 1965; Prime Minister 1968-69.

Tran Van Lam–19, 156
Leader of Citizens' Rally party 1955; Minister for Foreign Afairs 1969

Tran Van Minh–82
Minister for Defence 1965; C.-inC. February 1965.

Tran Van Soai–11, 15-16
Minister of State 1954; leader of Hoa Hao forces 1955.

Tran Van Tuyen–144, 155-156
Deputy Premier and Minister for Planning 1965; Chairman, National Salvation Front 1968-.

Tran Van Van–27-28, 76, 111, 115-116
Member of Committee for Progress and Liberty 1960; General Secretary, High National Council, September-December 1964; Chairman of People's and Armed Forces Council 1966; assassinated December 1966.

Trinh Dinh Thao–147, 151
Chairman, Alliance of National, Democratic and Peace Forces' Central Committee 1968-.

Trinh Minh Thé–11-12, 14-16
Caodaist leader, killed 1955.

Tri Quang, Thich–40, 90-91, 96, 98, 100-104, 132, 134-135
Leader of militant faction amongst Buddhists 1963 -; General Secretary, Higher Council of Buddhist order prior to 1966.

Truong Dinh Dzu – 126-127, 132, 134-135
Runner-up in 1967 presidential elections on a peace platform.
Vu Quoc Thuc – 34, 155
Minister of State 1968; Minister of State for post-war economy March 1969; Minister of State for Reconstruction and Development August 1969 -.
Vuong Van Duong – 28-29
Leader of attempted coup 1960.